THE BIG LIE ABOUT RACE
IN AMERICA'S SCHOOLS

SERIES | RACE AND EDUCATION

Series edited by H. Richard Milner IV

OTHER BOOKS IN THIS SERIES

THE BIG LIE ABOUT RACE
IN AMERICA'S SCHOOLS

Edited by
Royel M. Johnson
Shaun R. Harper

Harvard Education Press
Cambridge, Massachusetts

Paperback ISBN 9781682539132

Library of Congress Cataloging-in-Publication Data

Names: Johnson, Royel M., editor. | Harper, Shaun R., 1975– editor.
Title: The big lie about race in America's schools / edited by Royel M.
    Johnson, Shaun R. Harper.
Other titles: Race and education series.
Description: Cambridge, Massachusetts : Harvard Education Press, [2024] |
    Series: Race and education series | Includes bibliographical references
    and index.
Identifiers: LCCN 2024010212 | ISBN 9781682539132 (paperback)
Subjects: LCSH: Misinformation—Social aspects—United States. |
    Disinformation—Social aspects—United States. | Censorship—Social
    aspects—United States. | Democracy and education—United States. |
    Education and state—United States. | Educational leadership—United
    States.
Classification: LCC LC89 .B494 2024 | DDC 371.82900973—dc23/eng/20240515
LC record available at https://lccn.loc.gov/2024010212

Published by Harvard Education Press,
an imprint of the Harvard Education Publishing Group
Harvard Education Press
8 Story Street
Cambridge, MA 02138

Cover Design: Endpaper Studio

The typefaces in this book are Legacy Serif Std and Knockout.

We dedicate this book to courageous educators who teach full truths in our nation's K–12 schools and postsecondary institutions—even when doing so poses serious risks to their careers.

CONTENTS

SERIES FOREWORD

By H. Richard Milner IV
Race and Education series editor

A few years ago, a group of parents, community members, and policy advocates invited me to share recommendations from my research about ways to support minoritized communities in education. This diverse, but mostly white, group was concerned about racial unrest and potential local and broader backlash after the killing of George Floyd at the hand of the state. "Liberal minded," and "forward thinking" were how the group described themselves to me prior to and during my visit with them. I met with the group twice over Zoom prior to my presentation and discussion with them. The prepped me by sharing that they did not want to focus on race or the Floyd murder per se, but about poverty, economic disparities, drug addiction, and lack of opportunities for many in their community. They preferred, guided, and pleaded with me to prepare my talk for a much broader conversation about "minority groups" (in their words), and they wanted specific recommendations about ways to help students "do better" in schools. I was clear with the group that I would focus on a range of intersecting issues, but I also informed them that race would be central to the conversation. They pleaded: we must do something in our communities and especially our schools to quell the injustices communities were (and are) facing in society. Moreover, they were concerned about deep political divisions and lack of solidarity that seemed to be "tearing up" the United States of America (US).

Maintaining my professional obligation, ethical responsibility, and commitment to Truth-Telling, I prepared and focused my remarks on Black students, students living below the poverty line, students whose first language is not English, recent immigrant students, Muslim students, and LGBTQIA+ students. As promised during our meetings of preparation, I also attempted to focus on important and necessary intersections of these students' experiences and identities as I invited those in attendance to imagine and re-envision equitable advocacy, policies, and practices—informed by, processed through, and steeped in truth.

Drawing from well-substantiated research, I attempted to map and share with the group the complexities of the issues we face as a nation, sprinkled with recommendations on what they could (and should!) do in solidarity to make society and schools better. But it appeared that the group wanted simple, fixed, and definitive answers. As I presented, those in attendance engaged in sidebar conversations with and among each other reflecting on the data, insights, and recommendations I shared on slides. Although I could not hear their comments between and among them during my presentation, their concerns became clear after I finished my presentation. The very first comment from a participant (with head nods from most of the others in the room) was: This presentation feels like you are 'playing the race card.'"[1] A bit stunned and disappointed by the comment, my response was firm and resolute: "Yes, I certainly am," I countered: *"Play the race card."* In short, the authors in this book are Truth-Tellers; if readers of this book conclude with the idea that the recommendations are suggesting a "playing of the race card" to get at truth, then this is exactly what should be done. In the press for Truth, why should I or anyone committed to justice, equity, diversity, and inclusion placate toward white liberals or white conservatives or anyone supporting or advancing lies?

Those in my presentation's mostly white audience, self-described "liberals," wanted solutions disconnected from the *realness of racism*. From my view, they wanted suggestions and implications based on lies. Critical race theorist Derrick Bell has cautioned us against those fighting against what he called racial realism.[2] Indeed, Bell reminds us in his thesis of racial realism that Black and other communities of color cannot rely on white people through systems, institutions, organizations, laws, policies, or advocacy to transform the ugliness of racism in America.

The Big Lie About Race in America's Schools is just the book we need in this moment of lies, corruption, anti-justice, anti-diversity, anti-equity, and anti-democracy! Johnson and Harper have assembled a world-class cadre of colleagues to *name* the issues we face in education—pervasive and persistent lies. However, authors in this book not only outline the very areas that need to be considered in search of truth in American schools, but they outline ways to address and transform individual and systemic barriers that stifle progress toward racial justice. This edited book is rich across individual chapters and transformative as a collective volume. The book is a powerhouse collective of essays with deep interconnectedness, synergy, and coherence across chapters. For instance, drawing from well-established and substantiated research, authors in this volume:

- Counter, nuance, and confront the proliferation of misinformation about what is and should be taught in schools.
- Provide deep, rich, and robust implications and recommendations for schools and universities to organize and teach truth.
- Outline and discuss how politics and self-interests harm young people and educators inside and outside of P–12 schools and universities.
- Discuss what society must do to address a national crisis of lies meant to maintain white supremacy, patriarchy, and other forms of oppression.

This is a book for any of us committed to Truth-Telling and confronting the big lies that can undermine a democratic citizenry where young people have a fighting chance to learn from and through curriculum and instructional practices designed to help Americans know and learn from the past and press toward a democracy for all. Read this book.

PREFACE

In 2020, former US president Donald Trump created a massive conspiracy, "the Big Lie," to rationalize his failed reelection bid. This fictitious narrative, which has been supported by persistent disinformation and fake news, sought not only to dispute an electoral outcome, but to undermine and distort our very conception of truth. This playbook of deception, which relied heavily on baseless claims amplified across social media platforms as well as on Fox News Channel and other conservative news outlets, created an echo chamber. Claims about widespread voter fraud and electoral theft were repeated so often that they began to be accepted as truth by some constituents. However, ramifications of The Big Lie extended far beyond mere repudiation of the presidential election results; it amplified growing concerns about our country's direction among conservative constituents.

When white supremacists stormed the Capitol on January 6, 2021, to "make America great again," it was not at all surprising. Indeed, the insurrection marked the culmination of a trajectory of fears and frustrations, demonstrating how dangerous political rhetoric can ignite violent action. Thus,

The Big Lie became more than a political strategy—it emerged as a powerful tool for fostering distrust in institutions and distorting the fabric of reality. Today, conservative politicians, think tanks, and others have seized and are exploiting a similar strategy in their coordinated attacks on education. By leveraging anxieties about race relations and racial equity, they have distorted the narrative of what is being taught in classrooms, condemning it as "liberal indoctrination." Indeed, the new Big Lie in education amplifies deep-seated fears, painting an alarmist picture of an education system in which white students are unjustly blamed for historical wrongs and critical discussions about race and diversity are falsely portrayed as destructively divisive.

In this context, terms like "critical race theory" and "diversity, equity, and inclusion," or "DEI" have been weaponized, intentionally distorted from their original meanings and intent, and presented as reverse racism. This misrepresentation is a deliberate attempt to obfuscate the truth about the ongoing relevance of race and the pervasive influence of racism in our educational system and society. Understanding and confronting these issues are crucial for fostering an educational environment characterized by truth and for preparing students to navigate and transform a society where racial asymmetries are a significant and persistent reality.

The Big Lie About Race in America's Schools is a collective response to this challenge. This book brings together leading voices in education to dissect and counter misinformation and disinformation. We grapple with its implications for our K–12 schools, colleges, universities, and democracy. The authors explore the evolution of the politicized attack on racial truths in education, the tactics and logics underpinning it, its far-reaching consequences for students and educators, and strategies to counter it in pursuit of racial equity. A dozen chapters authored by experts spanning the P-20 education continuum provide insightful analyses on various facets of this national crisis—from the censorship of books to silencing and intimidation of teachers to legislative bans on DEI initiatives in colleges and universities.

Targeted at educators, policy makers, advocates, and all who are committed to upholding truth in education, this book serves as a vital resource. It is crafted for those who recognize the serious threats this deception poses to our democracy, as well as those who wish to act within their spheres of influence to counter them. The chapters are concise, focused, and practical. They individually and collectively offer clear, actionable insights and strategies for those seeking to navigate and transform the complex, racially charged terrain of contemporary educational contexts.

In the first chapter, Royel Johnson relies on a series of recent transformative events to contextualize the attacks on race and racial truth-telling in education. Drawing parallels with past efforts in the US to censor and obfuscate discussions of racial equity, he explains why these attacks are happening now. In chapter 2, Shaun Harper juxtaposes ten evidence-based truths about race in K–12 schools and higher education institutions with one big politicized lie about what is allegedly occurring in classrooms and on campuses across the country. John Pascarella III writes about book bans in chapter 3—why they are occurring, how educators and others are fighting back, and what more can be done to stop them.

In the next two chapters, Erica Silva offers guidance for teachers, and then Francesca López, Ashley Burns Nascimiento, and Elisa Serrano advise educational leaders on ways to resist The Big Lie.

In chapters 6 and 7, Jessica DeCuir-Gunby and Antonio Duran offer insights into the impact of The Big Lie in schools on Black children and queer students, respectively. Justin Coles then presents a compelling vision for the liberation of Black teachers who work in suppressive educational environments. In chapters 9 through 11, the authors offer countermeasures, resistant response strategies, shared leadership approaches, and critical policy moves that can be made in response to anti-DEI legislation and other efforts that aim to deny students access to the full truth about America's racial past and present. Shaun Harper forecasts in chapter 12 numerous long-term consequences of the contemporary attacks on truth-teaching. Finally, the book concludes with a chapter written by Jaleel Howard and Tyrone Howard that offers many forward-thinking, actionable things that can be done to sustain pursuits of racial justice and to defend our democracy.

As you prepare delve into this important text, we ask, Are you prepared to uphold the truth, the whole truth, and nothing but the truth about race and racism? The future of our democracy, the integrity of our educational institutions, and racial justice in our society depend on how you and others answer this consequential question. The task before us is not just to witness the realities of our students, educators, parents, and families, but also to actively engage with, validate, and elevate their historical and contemporary experiences.

When we do so, we reaffirm our commitment to education as a foundation to our democracy and as a critical site for truth in an age of misinformation and disinformation.

Royel M. Johnson
Shaun R. Harper
Los Angeles, California

CHAPTER I

"America Has a Problem"

Contextualizing the Attacks on Race and Racial Truth-Telling

Royel M. Johnson

The fourteenth track on Beyoncé's culture-shifting album, *Renaissance*, is boldly titled, "America Has a Problem." This infectious dance track generated quite a bit of buzz among fans and pundits who expected the same social and political consciousness-raising seen in her previous single, "Formation." You remember "Formation," right? It was the centerpiece song of her 2016 Super Bowl performance, which had far-right conservative talking heads, law enforcement, and social media in a frenzy, labeling it "un-American" and "antipolice." To our surprise, the lyrics of "America Has a Problem" describe a different kind of problem: Beyoncé herself. And there is no debate that she is indeed "That Girl." Okay, enough with the *Renaissance* references. Let's move on to more serious matters.

The song's title is a useful heuristic, as America indeed has a problem. It's a long-standing, wicked problem that continues to rear its ugly head time and again. A problem so intractable that, despite what often feels like Herculean milestones for racial progress, it puts us all back in our place (well, folks of color, at least), wielding its all-mighty power to undo and maintain the status quo. If it isn't clear already, we are talking about white supremacy: the ideologies and structures—social, political, economic, and otherwise—that create and sustain a racial hierarchy privileging and empowering whites at the expense, dehumanization, and exploitation of all other racial groups, but especially Black and Indigenous peoples.

Only in a white supremacist society could today's vicious and persistent attacks on race and racial truth-telling in schools and universities exist, with the deliberate distortion and omission of America's racial history. The political right's new boogeyman, critical race theory (CRT), is being used as a blanket term for all conversations and efforts related to understanding and addressing historic and contemporary racial inequities. Far-right conservatives use it to prey on the fears of whites about their potential loss of power and privilege, which white supremacy undeservedly affords them, and to distract the broader public from more insidious attacks underway.

Why are these attacks happening now? How do they fit in with past efforts in the US to censor and obfuscate racial equity and racial truth-telling? And why should we be concerned? These are the broad questions I explore in this chapter. In the following section, I chronicle the current attacks and take a closer look at what's really on the chopping block in the eighteen states that have enacted some form of restriction on how educators can teach about race and racism.

How Did We Get Here? The Evolution of the Anti-CRT/Racial Truth-Telling Movement

As of this writing, forty-four states have introduced bills or taken steps to place restrictions on how educators can teach about race/racism and other "divisive concepts" since January 2021. Eighteen of these states have imposed those bans through legislation or other state-level action, according to *Education Week* (see table 1.1), which has been tracking these educational gag orders.[1] How did we get here? Let's look back at some of the events leading up to the flurry of anti-CRT/truth-telling bills (see figure 1.1).

New York Times' *1619 Project*

The launch of the *New York Times'* 1619 Project was a significant spark that ignited the flames for the series of attacks on CRT and racial truth-telling. Developed by *New York Times* staff writer and Pulitzer Prize winner, Nikole Hannah-Jones, the 1619 Project is a long-form multimedia project that aims to "reframe the country's history by placing the consequences of slavery and contributions of Black Americans at the very center of the United States' national narrative."[2]

Launched in August 2019 to mark the 400th anniversary of the origin of American slavery, the project shifts focus to a less notable date in our country's history: the year 1619. Historical records indicate that in late August 1619, a ship carrying roughly twenty to thirty enslaved Africans arrived at Point Comfort in the British colony of Virginia. This event, the *New York Times* argues, marks the inauguration a

Table 1.1 State-level legislative bans on critical race theory and related topics

Pending[a]	No state action	Passed	Failed
NC	CA	AL	AK
NJ	DC	AR	AZ
	DE	FL	CO
	HI	GA	CT
	MA	IA	IL
	NV	ID	IN
	VT	KY	KS
		MS	LA
		MT	MD
		ND	ME
		NH	MI
		OK	MN
		SC	MO
		SD	NE
		TN	NM
		TX	NY
		UT	OH
		VA	OR
			PA
			RI
			WA
			WI
			WV
			WY

Source: Education Week (2023)
[a]As of June 13, 2023.

barbaric system of chattel slavery that would endure for over 250 years.[3] The 1619 Project counters dominant narratives about America's founding and birth year (i.e., 1776) by placing slavery and the contributions of Black Americans at the center of American history. It insists that the enslavement of Black Americans is a fundamental part of the foundation and expansion of America, with consequences that continue to reverberate for Black Americans today.

The project began with a series of essays published in a special issue of the *New York Times*, covering a range of issues from mass incarceration to the wealth gap and medical inequality. Shortly afterward, it was announced that the Pulitzer Center was partnering with the 1619 Project to produce free, original curricular materials and resources for school and university educators.[4] According to the Pulitzer Center's 2019 annual report, more than 3,500 classrooms in all fifty states are using the curricular materials, including five school districts in Buffalo, New York; Chicago, Illinois; Washington, DC; Wilmington, Delaware; and Winston-Salem, North Carolina.[5] This number has likely increased considerably, given the partnership's expansion over the past three years, including a national education network, on-demand professional development for educators, and a national annual meeting.

Criticism of the 1619 Project was inevitable. Northwestern University professor of history Dr. Leslie Harris published an essay in Politico titled, "I Helped Fact-Check the 1619 Project. The Times Ignored Me."[6] Her primary concern was that Nikole Hannah-Jones's essay misrepresented the colonies' motivation to fight for independence (i.e., preservation of slavery). Professor Harris feared such an overstatement would be weaponized to discredit the entire project, which she described overall as a "much-needed corrective to the blindly celebratory histories that once dominated our understanding of the past—histories that wrongly suggested racism and slavery were not a central part of U.S history."[7] She was not wrong about this.

In addition to criticism by notable white historians about its factual errors,[8] conservative groups, politicians, and academics accused the project of fueling race division and hatred, promoting leftist ideology and indoctrination, and being revisionist history.[9] These arguments were marshaled just one month later when Republican Senator Tom Cotton of Arizona introduced the Saving American History Act of 2020, which aims to reduce federal funding to public schools that teach *The New York Times'* 1619 Project.[10] A national "racial reckoning" soon ensued in response to highly publicized killings of Black people.

Anti-Black Police Killings, #BlackLivesMatter, and Summer 2020 "Racial Reckoning"

On February 23, 2020, Ahmaud Arbery, a twenty-five-year-old Black man went for a jog in Satilla Shores, a neighborhood in Glynn County, Georgia. He was chased down and killed by three white men who erroneously assumed he was a burglar. Several weeks later, on March 13, 2020, Breonna Taylor, a twenty-six-year-old Black woman, was killed by Louisville police officers who stormed her apartment to serve a no-knock warrant. Taylor, an emergency medical technician (EMT), was asleep at the time of the raid, with her boyfriend, Kenneth Walker. Out of fear, Walker fired a warning shot at police officers, who he assumed were intruders. The officers fired thirty-two shots in return, six of which struck and killed Taylor.

On Memorial Day, May 25, 2020, a forty-six-year-old Black man by the name of George Floyd was killed in Minneapolis, Minnesota. Floyd was arrested by a police officer after a store clerk accused him of purchasing cigarettes with counterfeit money. Despite Floyd's repeated declaration, "I can't breathe," white police officer Derek Chauvin applied his knee to Floyd's neck and back for nine minutes and twenty-three seconds, resulting in his death. The painful-to-watch video of Floyd circulated quickly, racking up millions of views from folks around the world. His state-sanctioned, public execution, (re)ignited long-standing concerns about racism in policing, as well as broader issues around race and racism in our social, political, and economic systems.

The names of Floyd, Arbery, and Taylor, along with dozens of others who have been otherwise rendered invisible by public media, became part of the rallying cry of protesters around the world who mobilized to declare that #BlackLivesMatter in the summer of 2020. Founded in 2013 in response to the acquittal of George Zimmerman, who murdered Trayvon Martin, #BlackLivesMatter is a global organization with a mission "to eradicate white supremacy and build local power to intervene in violence inflicted on Black communities by the state and vigilantes."[11]

Public support for the #BlackLivesMatter protests grew rapidly across partisan and racial lines. Indeed, something felt *different* about the moment. According to political pundits and talking heads, a "racial reckoning" was underway. And for some, it seemed so. National conversations about efforts to defund police city departments emerged;[12] corporations pledged $200 billion to racial justice initiatives;[13] college and university leaders announced initiatives to increase faculty and student diversity;[14] and confederate flags and symbols around the country were being removed.[15] While these were meaningful gestures, they fell short of the kind of structural reforms that can produce long-term, material impact for Black Americans. More on this later.

Trump's Executive Order

In July 2020, an employee of the city of Seattle documented an anti-bias training session they participated in and shared screenshots of PowerPoint slides with a local journalist and filmmaker, Christopher F. Rufo, who recognized and seized it as a political opportunity.[16] Through a public records request, he obtained and published examples of the slides and curricula that were used on his website in an essay titled "Separate but Unequal." He observes, "Under the banner of 'antiracism,' Seattle's Office of Civil Rights is now explicitly endorsing principles of segregationism, group-based guilt, and race essentialism—ugly concepts that should have been left behind a century ago."[17]

In a conversation with a reporter at the *New Yorker*, Rufo states that conservatives need a new language to describe the culture war and fight against progressive racial ideology. CRT, he points out, was the "perfect villain." He is quoted, saying "Its [CRT] connotations are all negative to most middle-class Americans, including racial minorities, who see the world as 'creative' rather than 'critical,' 'individual' rather than 'racial,' 'practical' rather than 'theoretical.' Strung together, the phrase 'critical race theory' connotes hostile, academic, divisive, race-obsessed, poisonous, elitist, anti-American."[18] Rufo adds that what makes CRT perfect is that it is not "an externally applied pejorative." Instead, "it's the label the critical race theorists chose themselves."

On September 1, 2020, Rufo appeared on Fox News for a televised interview with Tucker Carlson, during which he called on then-President Trump to immediately issue an executive order (EO) that abolishes CRT training in the federal government, describing it as an "existential threat to the United States."[19] Several days later, Trump retweeted Rufo's appearance on Fox, and he responded with "Not any more!" to a tweet from someone who wrote that "critical race theory is the greatest threat to western civilization and it's made its way into the US federal government." In a separate tweet, Trump called CRT "a sickness that cannot be allowed to continue."[20]

Just days later, on September 4, 2020, Russell Vought, the then-director of the Office of Management and Budget, issued a memo to all heads of executive departments and agencies to cease and desist federal resources to fund "divisive, un-American propaganda training sessions."[21] Subsequently, on September 22, 2020, Trump officially signed EO 13950 into law, which effectively prohibited the inclusion or mention of "divisive concepts," which he referred to as notions that

- one race or sex is inherently superior to another race or sex;
- the United States is fundamentally racist or sexist;
- an individual, by virtue of his or her race or sex, is inherently racist, sexist, or oppressive, whether consciously or unconsciously;
- an individual should be discriminated against or receive adverse treatment solely or partly because of his or her race or sex;
- members of one race or sex cannot and should not attempt to treat others without respect to race or sex;
- an individual's moral character is necessarily determined by his or her race or sex;
- an individual, by virtue of his or her race or sex, bears responsibility for actions committed in the past by other members of the same race or sex;

- any individual should feel discomfort, guilt, anguish, or any other form of psychological distress on account of his or her race or sex; or
- meritocracy or traits such as a hard work ethic are racist or sexist, or were created by a particular race to oppress another race.[22]

The nine divisive concepts outlined in Trump's EO are important, as they have formed the basis for the flurry of state bills banning CRT and racial truth-telling. Following EO 13950, in November, Trump also signed EO 13958, which established the 1776 Commission, an eighteen-person committee appointed by the president to write a report on "core principles of the American founding and how these principles may be understood to further enjoyment of "the blessings of liberty."[23] The Commission, an obvious response to the 1619 Project, aimed to address supposed distortions of America's history and promote "patriotic education."

January 6 Insurrection

Shortly following Trump's EO, white supremacy reared its head once again, this time at our nation's capitol, in front of cameras and for the world to see. After the defeat of former US President Donald Trump in the 2020 presidential election, thousands of angry white mobsters stormed the US Capitol, in support of Trump. They displayed Confederate flags, used racial slurs, hung nooses, and carried other symbols associated with anti-Semitism and white supremacist ideologies. The election of Biden appeared to heighten the anxieties of some white Americans, prompting them to quickly mobilize, taking to the capital to "Make America Great Again."

Copycat Legislation: January 2021 Onward

Recall that since January 2021, eighteen states have imposed educational gag orders that suppress racial truth-telling in schools (see table 1.2). By late June 2021, seven states had taken action, with Idaho being the first to pass state legislation through House Bill (HB) 388. The bill copies language from the divisive concepts included in Trump's EO and erroneously labels them "tenets of Critical Race Theory" that "exacerbate and inflame divisions based on sex, race, ethnicity, religion, color, national origin, or other criteria in ways contrary to the unity of the nation and well-being of the state of Idaho and its citizens."[24] Similarly, Montana's attorney general, Austin Knudsen, issued a legally binding opinion at the behest of the superintendent of public instruction, Elsie Arntzen, describing "antiracism" as a "rhetorical weapon."[25] The opinion includes a laundry list of restrictions, such as students questioning their privilege through activities like the privilege walk.

The second wave of educational gag orders was passed from early August through early November in Alabama, Utah, and North Dakota (see figure 1.1). In Alabama, for example, the State Board of Education adopted a resolution that prohibits schools from teaching "concepts that impute fault, blame, a tendency to oppress others, or the need to feel guilt or anguish to persons solely because of their race or sex." Similarly, North Dakota broadly prohibits the teaching of CRT, with limited clarification about its content beyond acknowledging that racism is embedded in America's social and legal system.

In 2022, eight more educational gag orders were imposed, starting with Virginia, where newly elected Republican Governor Glenn Youngkin signed an EO on his first day in office.

Table 1.2 Overview of educational gag orders

State	Date signed	Bill number	Target institution	Types of restrictions	"Divisive concepts"
Idaho	4/29/21	HB 377	K-12	Curricular content	Yes
Tennessee	5/25/21	SB 623	K-12	Classroom teaching; curricular content	Yes
Arkansas	5/3/21	SB 627/Act 1100	K12; higher education; contractors: private businesses/nonprofit	Classroom teaching; trainings	Yes
Oklahoma	5/7/21	HB 1775	K-12; higher education	Classroom teaching; curricular content; trainings	Yes
Montana	5/27/21	Legal Opinion by AG	K-12; higher education	Classroom teaching; curricular content	Yes
Texas	6/15/21	HB 3979	K-12	Classroom teaching; curricular content; trainings	Yes
South Carolina	6/3/21	H4100	K-12	Classroom teaching; trainings	Yes
Iowa	6/8/21	HF 802	K-12; higher education; contractors: private businesses/nonprofit	Classroom teaching; curricular content; trainings	Yes
New Hampshire	6/25/21	HB2	K-12; contractors; private businesses/nonprofit	Classroom teaching; trainings	Yes

State	Date	Measure	Scope	Description	Enforcement
Alabama	8/12/21	Resolution	K-12	Classroom teaching; curricular content; trainings	Yes
Utah	8/9/21	Rule	K-12	Classroom teaching; curricular content; trainings	Yes
North Dakota	11/12/21	HB 1508	K-12	Classroom teaching; curricular content	Yes
Virginia	1/15/22	EO	K-12	Classroom teaching; curricular content	Yes
Mississippi	3/14/22	SB 2113	K-12; higher education	Classroom teaching	Yes
Tennessee	4/8/22	HB 2670	Higher education	Training	Yes
Florida	4/22/22	HB 7	K-12; higher education; private businesses/nonprofit	Curricular content; trainings	Yes
South Dakota	4/5/22	EO 2022-02	K-12	Classroom teaching; curricular content; trainings	Yes
Georgia	4/28/22	HB 1084	K-12	Classroom teaching; curricular content; trainings	Yes
Kentucky	4/13/22	SB 1	K-12	Classroom teaching; curricular content; trainings	No
South Dakota	3/21/22	HB 1012	K-12; higher education	Classroom teaching; curricular content	Yes
Arkansas	1/10/23	EO	K-12; private businesses/nonprofit	Classroom teaching; curricular content; trainings	Yes

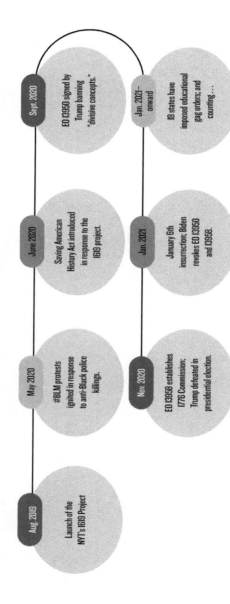

Figure 1.1 Timeline of events leading to educational gag orders

In addition to prohibiting "divisive concepts, including Critical Race Theory" in schools, the EO instructs the superintendent of instruction to conduct an internal review of state policies and practices that may promote "divisive concepts" such as its cultural competency training and school curriculum. In April 2022, Florida Governor Ron DeSantis signed the controversial "Stop W.O.K.E. Act,"[26] which stands for "Wrong to Our Kids and Employees." As the name suggests, the bill aims to address what it terms "woke indoctrination" in schools and businesses by prohibiting instruction and training that might result in students or employees feeling that they bear "personal responsibility" for historical wrongdoings because of their race, sex, or national origin.[27]

In nearly every instance of state legislation or legal action, there is language that is identical to or heavily paraphrased from Trump's September 2020 EO. This is not surprising, given that the Heritage Foundation produced a model bill for state lawmakers to use for prohibiting CRT in K–12 schools, which also draws on language from Trump's EO. The Foundation publicly cites and praises Mississippi, Arizona, Georgia, and South Carolina for using their model legislation.[28] If it is not clear already, this is a well-coordinated and funded movement—one that enables conservatives to hone a consistent message in their attacks across states.

While the first wave of educational gag orders primarily focused on K–12 schools, there is an increased focus on colleges and universities as well. Eight of eighteen states with gag orders in place have a focus on public institutions of higher education. Both Texas and Florida, for instance, have enacted legislation that imposes periodic tenure reviews or the elimination of tenure to "depoliticize the classroom."[29] We should be very concerned about such efforts. This is why PEN America and the American Association of Colleges and Universities (AAC&U) issued a joint statement noting that these legislative restrictions "infringe upon freedom of speech and academic freedom, [and constrain] vital societal discourse on pressing questions relating to American history, society, and culture."[30]

What is also striking about the educational gag orders imposed by the eighteen states is their vacuous, contradictory, ambiguous, and in some cases, egregious factual errors. Consider HB 1040 in Indiana, which requires that teachers lead "impartial discussion of controversial aspects of history."[31] In that same bill, teachers are required to instruct students that "socialism, Marxism, communism, totalitarianism, or similar political systems are incompatible with and in conflict with the principles of freedom upon which the United States was founded." One consequence of noncompliance is termination. Please make it make sense.

Deja Vu: How History Repeats Itself

We have all heard some version of the quote, "Those who don't know their history are doomed to repeat it." It is a popular saying that is widely used, though its source is debatable. That far-right conservatives aim to suppress America's vitriolic history of racial terror and oppression should be concerning. Such strategic tactics are not new or novel, though. Indeed, it is history that provides a sobering reminder of similar efforts.

Can you imagine if educators around the country were required to recite and sign loyalty oaths to pledge their allegiance to the government and to disavow association with organizations or groups that support CRT and the 1619 Project? Let us imagine. Repeat after me:

> I, [Your Name], do solemnly swear (or affirm) that I will not advocate for, teach, or promote Critical Race Theory (CRT) or any related curriculum that explores systemic racial inequities, historical or contemporary, in my capacity as an educator at [Insert Your Institution]. I further disavow any association with organizations or movements that seek to address or highlight racial injustices through education or advocate for the restructuring of societal institutions to address racial inequality. I commit to refraining from engaging in discussions or teachings that could be construed as divisive or that challenge the narrative of racial neutrality and equality without regard to the historical and ongoing impacts of racism in the United States.

This idea isn't far-fetched, and is one that we should be concerned about. If you were an educator in California during the 1950s, you would have had to recite and sign a loyalty oath that read like this:

> I do solemnly swear (or affirm) that I am not a member of the Communist Party or any other organization which advocates the overthrow of the Government by force or violence; that I have not, within five years preceding the taking of this oath, been a member of any organization which advocates the overthrow of the Government by force or violence; and that I am not affiliated with any organization which teaches or advocates the overthrow of the Government by force or violence, or with any person who advocates such overthrow of the Government.

Due in part to concerns and paranoia about the rise of communism, the California State Legislature enacted the Levering Act in 1950, which, as you can see, required state employees, including educators, to disavow affiliation with and sympathy for communism. The Levering Act was part of a broader national trend in response to federal government efforts, led by Republican Senator Joseph McCarthy, to address alleged communists within the government that threatened "the American Way." What is the American Way? Do you mean any effort, information, or ideas that challenge, critique, or aim to foster awareness about deep-seated power asymmetries that oppress and relegate some at the expense of others?

It was not just loyalty oaths, though. Teachers suspected of being communist sympathizers were aggressively investigated and surveilled. Some were blacklisted from teaching or working in education altogether, which had negative material consequences for their livelihood. Public smear campaigns in the media and other shaming tactics were used. Does any of this sound familiar or at all probable today?

Far-right conservatives have effectively fostered a climate of fear for educators and have normalized retaliation. We need to look no further than Nikole Hannah-Jones, the brain behind the 1619 Project, who was denied tenure in 2021 at the University of North Carolina (UNC) at Chapel Hill despite unanimous support from faculty colleagues after the university's board of trustees expressed concern about her "divisive" and "un-American" scholarship. In Tennessee, a white man teacher who taught his students about white privilege was fired.[32] In another instance, a Florida teacher was fired for hanging a #BlackLivesMatter poster over her classroom door and rewarding student activism.[33] And in North Texas, a Black man principal at a mostly white high school resigned after facing accusations that he was indoctrinating students with CRT.[34] This is after he issued a letter to the school community in 2020 following the brutal murders of George Floyd, Breonna Taylor, and Ahmaud Arbery describing his hurt.

Ibram X. Kendi, historian and author of one of the most banned books in the United States, "How to be An Antiracist," notes that "the only way to undo racism is to consistently identify and describe it—and then dismantle it."[35] Naming racism requires knowledge and awareness. It requires history—the kind of racial history that eighteen states have imposed educational gag orders suppress. In no uncertain terms, America does have a problem. This problem is not new, though. And if we are not careful (it doesn't appear that we are), we are doomed to repeat the mistakes that the 1619 Project and other efforts aim to educate us about.

Ten Truths and One Very Big Lie About Racial Realities in K–12 Schools and Higher Education Institutions

Shaun R. Harper

Joe Biden won the 2020 presidential election. Insisting he did not is one of the biggest, most divisive, and chaos-igniting lies in American history. Months before the election occurred, then-president Donald Trump exclaimed that the only way he would not be reelected was if there was electoral fraud.[1] He said this before any voter mailed in a ballot or entered a voting booth. It was a dangerous and outrageous claim that lacked evidence, which is why it has since become referred to as "The Big Lie." Its education counterpart similarly emerged from a set of claims that lack sufficient proof. Manufacturers and disseminators of The Big Lie in schools claim that curricula and teaching practices, like Trump's re-election, are rigged to disadvantage American citizens. Both lies were popularized during roughly the same timeframe. One motive unifies them: divisive partisan politics.

The Select Committee to Investigate the January 6th Attack on the United States Capitol, the courts, state election certifiers, media outlets, and even Trump's own lawyers found very few election irregularities, a number that cannot be legitimately characterized as widespread voter fraud.[2] Even when they were furnished with credible evidence, election deniers still insisted that Trump secured more votes than Biden in 2020. Racism deniers are similarly rejecting facts about what is actually occurring in K–12 schools and on college campuses across the country. Decontextualized screenshots of PowerPoint slides, along with video and audio snippets from a very small handful of bad diversity, equity, and inclusion (DEI) presentations, are being politically misrepresented as examples of what is occurring everywhere. Governors, state legislators, and school board members are banning trainings in which they themselves have not participated, curriculum and lessons they have not reviewed, and books they have not read. Such actions are analogous to Trump declaring fraud in an election that had not yet commenced.

It is important to counter The Big Lie about race in education with data. Hence, I provide numerous facts in this chapter. Specifically, I draw on nearly two decades of qualitative and quantitative research on campus racial climates at more than two hundred colleges and universities in every geographic region of the country. I also leverage data collected from thousands of educators who have participated in my center's professional learning programs over the past four years. Additionally, I use statistics from the US Department of Education and other organizations to disprove unfounded assumptions about what educators are doing in the name of racial equity. Beyond presenting truths, I also highlight some logic flaws in the misinformation and disinformation that is being used to mislead the American public. Altogether, I present ten data-informed truths. This chapter then concludes with one ginormous lie about race in K–12 schools and postsecondary institutions.

Truth 1: There Are Serious Racial Problems on Campuses

The USC Race and Equity Center, which I founded and direct, designs and delivers rigorous, evidenced-based, and high-quality professional learning experiences for educators in K–12 schools and districts, colleges, and universities across the US. Thousands of education professionals annually participate in our programs. On average, 94 percent of participants deem our educational sessions practically useful and 95 percent deem them excellent. We do not teach educators critical race theory (CRT) or aim to indoctrinate them with so-called divisive concepts. We do, however, create productive spaces for them to be honest about the realities of race on campuses.

One way we do this is through anonymous polling. Take, for instance, our alliance of seventy-one liberal arts colleges across the country. In a live three-hour session on Zoom, I launched a poll that asked hundreds of faculty members, staff, and administrators from Alliance member institutions (the overwhelming majority of whom were white) if there were serious racial problems on their campuses. Eighty-four percent said yes, seven percent said they were unsure, and the remaining few said no. I have posed this same question in dozens of learning sessions with K–12 and higher education professionals over the past four years. Almost always, at least 70 percent of participants anonymously report that their institutions have serious racial problems.

At an in-person event for eighty principals across the Los Angeles Unified School District, we created a brave space for attendees to share examples of racial problems in their schools. Many of the examples they offered were horrifying. I have no reason to believe the stories these school leaders shared were in any way fictitious or exaggerated. In many ways, they were consistent with what I have heard and continue to hear from educators and administrators elsewhere. My center colleagues and I treat what practitioners tell us is happening on their campuses as data. When they say there are serious racial problems, we choose to believe them. Proponents of The Big Lie would likely mischaracterize these educators as being too "woke"—meaning they are radical justice-seekers who refuse to remain oblivious to or silent about racism and other forms of inequity, disrespect and disregard, violence, and human suffering. It is clear to me that acknowledging truths about race and seeking guidance on ways to address racial inequities—not wokeness—are almost always the motives of educators who bravely share examples of serious racial problems at their institutions.

Truth 2: Teachers Too Often Do Racist Things

Wearing blackface to school to teach a lesson about Black history. Assigning Black students the role of slaves and casting their white peers as slave masters during field trips to plantations. Placing slave trading math questions on quizzes. Referring to students, parents, and community members as niggers. Being photographed at school holding a noose. Dressing up on Halloween as immigration officers who seek to deport border-crossing Mexican immigrants. These are just a small handful of racist things that white teachers and school leaders have done in recent years. James Bridgeforth, one of my former doctoral advisees, handcrafted a database of 538 educator-involved racist incidents that occurred in K–12 schools between 2014 and 2019.[3] These are not microaggressions or incidents that could be left open to interpretation—everything in Bridgeforth's database is incontestably racist. They are also factual, meaning they actually occurred. Hence, they are evidence of racial problems in schools. To be sure, incidents like those that Bridgeforth meticulously catalogued are not confined to K–12 schools. *Inside Higher Ed*, a national daily news source, frequently publishes stories about faculty and staff members doing and saying racist things on college campuses. They use evidence to substantiate their reporting about racist encounters and other racial problems.

Truth 3: Too Many People of Color Experience Racism on Campuses

I have been conducting research on campus racial climates since 2005. For most of those years, my research team members and I have employed qualitative methods to understand the realities and complexities of race on campuses. We have conducted in-person interviews with more than ten thousand people at colleges and universities across the US. Consistently,

Black students tell us that white peers and employees on their campuses call them niggers. At one community college we studied, Black custodial workers were continually greeted with monkey sounds on walkie talkies; coworkers put bananas in their lockers one day to further reinforce the racist notion that they were monkeys, not people. Black collegians and employees have shared numerous examples of having the police called on them because white peers presumed they were criminal trespassers.

Predominantly white fraternities hold blackface parties. Black women are denied membership to predominantly white sororities because of their race. Nooses are hung on the front doors of Black culture centers. Racist, threatening emails are sent to Black faculty members. These are just a few examples of the stories Black people have told me in interviews over the years. Asian American, Indigenous, Latinx, and Pacific Islander students and employees also have offered heartbreaking examples of racism they have experienced on campuses.

In 2019, the USC Race and Equity Center launched the National Assessment of Collegiate Campus Climates (NACCC), a suite of quantitative surveys that have since been administered to more than two million students, faculty, and staff members all across the US. NACCC results corroborate many of our qualitative findings: for instance, students of color experience higher rates of racist incidents on campuses than do their white peers. NACCC data also further confirm what employees anonymously report in our professional learning programs: that their campuses have serious racial problems. While my center has not conducted research on the racial climate in K–12 educational contexts, Bridgeforth's aforementioned database provides far too many examples of racist school climates.

I often invite participants in my center's professional learning sessions to anonymously describe times they either experienced firsthand, observed, or heard about racist situations that occurred at their institutions. Here are five examples from K–12 employees:

Someone scrawled "Ms. [Teacher's Name] is an ugly nigger with yellow teeth!" on the wall of the boys' restroom.

While walking in a hallway, a parent said, "You are just a nigger." This parent was angry that a teacher did not change her kid's grade and felt that I, the administrator, should have overruled the teacher.

I witnessed a police officer grab and slam a Black student down on her seat because he did not like her attitude. The student was already in handcuffs and seated in a chair. The student knew I was standing nearby and yelled for me to help. I raised my voice at the officer and it only pissed him off. I did not care. I defended the student and myself.

Two mothers got into an argument at dismissal. They were both yelling at each other with equal vigor. One mother, who was Latina, flagged down a police officer, who proceeded to arrest the Black mother because the other mother felt threatened by her.

I happened upon a framed map of the school in which the dean had labeled the lunch areas by the groups of students who hung out there. The labels were all racial slurs . . . other school personnel thought the map was a joke and had not thought it was an act of racism until they saw how offended I was by it.

And here are four examples from employees across higher education institutions:

> Faculty member taking off a student's hijab in class saying that he needed to know it was actually her that was going to take a test.

> A Latina student walked into an advanced math class and the professor asked, 'are you in the right class?'

> A faculty member allowed a student to present in black-face, even after a Black student shared with that instructor that they were uncomfortable. The faculty union defended the faculty member's decision.

> I am regularly called by the name of every other Black female faculty by other faculty. I've been [mistakenly] congratulated for tenure, on a stage, publicly at a campus-wide welcome event for three years in a row—the first time, I was even recognized as a part of the wrong division.

These nine examples are neither isolated nor wildly dissimilar to the nearly one thousand others that educators and administrators have anonymously submitted in my sessions over the past three years. Collectively, they confirm that racist incidents continue to occur in K–12 schools and on college campuses.

Truth 4: Most Educators and Leaders Are White

US Department of Education data show that nearly 80 percent of all public K–12 school teachers are white and 77 percent are women.[4] Where is the evidence that lots of woke white women are teaching racist concepts to preschool, elementary, middle, and high school students? Federal data also show that 69 percent of full-time assistant, associate, and full professors at postsecondary institutions are white; 60 percent of those are white men.[5] There are more white male faculty members across these three ranks than there are faculty of color and women combined. Given that they comprise such a significant majority, could it be white guys who are making classrooms racially uncomfortable for white students? Are they the indoctrinators? Where is the proof?

Underlying the Big Lie in education is the idea that white students and employees are being systematically discriminated against. But little stocktaking is done of who the discriminators are. For instance, data from the College and University Professional Association for Human Resources show that nearly 70 percent of admissions coordinators and counselors are white.[6] Among vice presidents, deans, directors, and heads of admission, 78 percent are white. This suggests that most of the people who allegedly engage in so-called reverse discrimination against white applicants are themselves white. Really?

In 2022, a Texas A&M associate professor filed a highly publicized class action lawsuit against his university for alleged discrimination against white and Asian applicants for faculty jobs.[7] At the time, whites comprised 62.6 percent of the Texas A&M faculty, according to the University's Fall 2022 Workforce Profile.[8] Were they the discriminators? Could it be that the 3.8 percent of Black and 7.0 percent of Latino faculty had somehow amassed enough power to systematically lock white applicants out of professorships across academic schools and departments? In my campus racial climate research, faculty of color say they do not have such power and authority, especially given their severe underrepresentation in tenured professorships, department chair roles, and deanships. Hence, I do not believe them to be the predominant discriminators at Texas A&M and at other universities where such unfounded, illogical claims are made.

Truth 5: Most Educators Avoid Talking About Race

In the K–12 schools with which I have worked over the years, most teachers and educational leaders have described workplace cultures in which conversations about race are deliberately avoided. This is consistent with what employees at postsecondary institutions have reported in interviews my research team members and I have conducted with them for qualitative campus racial climate studies. In "Nine Themes in Campus Racial Climates and Implications for Institutional Transformation," my most-cited publication, Sylvia Hurtado and I noted that race was treated as a taboo topic on campuses at that time.[9] Reportedly, that continues to be the case. Across all levels, today's educators say they do not talk about race because they do not know how to do so comfortably, confidently, and productively. In virtual and in-person workshops with educators, I often give participants opportunities to anonymously pose questions they have long had about something pertaining to race at their current institutions but for some reason have not felt comfortable asking aloud. I have collected more than three thousand questions over the past decade. Here are a dozen that were perceivably unaskable:

- Is it Black, African American, or both?
- Why aren't our faculty and senior leadership more diverse?
- Is it okay to ask someone how they identify racially?
- How does it feel to be the only person of color in our department?
- Why are janitors the only Hispanic people who work here?

- How can I better support you as a Black woman?
- How can I as a white woman lead conversations on race?
- Why do we struggle to hire diverse candidates?
- How can we address implicit biases within hiring committees?
- Will I get in trouble if I post a Black Lives Matter sign in my office window?
- Would you honestly tell me if I said or did something racially insensitive?
- Why do we leave Asian Americans out of conversations about race?

Honestly, I think of these as important, yet relatively low-stakes, racial queries. They do not feel explosive to me. Notwithstanding, they are examples of what does not get talked about in many K–12 and postsecondary educational workplaces.

White educators and administrators confess that they stay away from questions like these because they are terrified of being labeled racist if they unintentionally say something that offends their colleagues. Professionals of color say they often avoid talking about race at work because they fear retaliation. They do not want to be labeled the "angry" person of color who makes their white colleagues uncomfortable with unwanted race talk. And in many instances, they say they opt out because they are tired of always being expected to lead difficult, at times awkward conversations about race. So then, is it possible that educators who avoid talking about race and racism with their colleagues are comfortably engaging these topics with students? If they are not willing to ask questions like the dozen I listed here, I seriously doubt they are posing higher-level, more controversial questions in classrooms.

Truth 6: Most Educators Don't Know How to Teach About Race

With a grant from the Bill & Melinda Gates Foundation, my USC Rossier School of Education faculty colleague John Pascarella III and I created an eight-session professional learning series for colleagues who teach at other schools of education throughout California. Hundreds of faculty members joined us from eighteen California State University campuses, nine University of California campuses, the Stanford Graduate School of Education, the USC Rossier School of Education, and twenty-four other higher education institutions across our state. In designing the series, Pascarella and I recognized that professors in teacher preparation programs cannot teach aspiring K–12 teachers things about race that they themselves never learned. We also understood that these faculty colleagues are complicit, oftentimes unintentionally, in sustaining and exacerbating educational inequities when they send underprepared graduates of their programs into K–12 schools with insufficient racial literacy.

The presumptions that informed the design of our series were neither arbitrary nor theoretical. They came from our prior work with K–12 teachers throughout California and across the nation who over the years had consistently confessed to us that they learned too little about race in college and graduate school. Our analyses of curricula across schools of education largely explain this. Few courses that are explicitly about race and racism exist in university-based teacher preparation programs. One obligatory "multicultural education" course that includes a week or two on race is much more common. Meaningfully and measurably integrating racial topics across the curriculum, while ideal, rarely occurs in most teacher preparation programs. Consequently, new professionals enter K–12 classrooms not knowing what to do. Many tell my research team members and me that this is another reason they attempt to avoid engaging racial topics with their colleagues and students. They and others also inadvertently make racial mistakes in classrooms.

I do an exercise with educators in K–12 and postsecondary contexts across the nation—including my own faculty colleagues when I was a professor at the University of Pennsylvania Graduate School of Education—that helps participants recognize their clumsiness with race. I give every educator a blank note card and four instructions: (1) write as legibly as your abilities allow, (2) do not write your name anywhere on the note card, (3) do not disclose anyone else's name in what you write, and (4) succinctly describe a time you made a racial mistake or otherwise mishandled teaching about race in your classroom. Almost always, every note card I get back has a substantive example written on it. We then talk through why those situations occurred, how they could have been better handled, what could be learned from them, and how they can be avoided in the future. As we debrief the exercise at the end, most educators say that no space had been previously created for them to name and learn from racial mistakes they had made.

Truth 7: Most Administrators Never Learned How To Solve Racial Problems

I conducted a multiyear qualitative study of 138 master's and doctoral students who were enrolled in higher education, student affairs, and community college leadership programs across fourteen mostly top-ranked schools of education. I also interviewed recent graduates of those programs who were within their first five years of full-time work as practitioners. When I asked what they learned about race in graduate school, most said they were introduced to racial identity theories in their one student development course. Similar to students who take the one multicultural education course in K–12 teacher preparation programs, participants in my study said they spent a week or two on race in their diversity in higher education course (which was usually an elective) before having to swiftly move on to gender, religion, socioeconomic status, sexual orientation, and other diversity topics. Most said they occasionally learned about the existence of racial inequities through readings they were assigned, but they were never taught what to do about those inequities or how to actually solve racial problems in practice. These findings have been corroborated over and over again in my work with K–12 and higher education administrators. In my center's professional learning programs, I often explicitly ask practitioners if they recall ever learning about the topics we are covering when they were in college or graduate school. "No" or "not nearly enough" are the typical responses.

Having been denied prior educational opportunities to engage with case studies and to rehearse leadership responses, K–12 and postsecondary administrators are typically caught by surprise when overt racism happens on campus. Few know what to do. Consequently, their actions often disappoint students who were targeted, as well as their parents and family members. There is one thing that leaders usually do when racial catastrophes erupt: they write statements that miss the mark. Take for example, a racist incident that targeted

Black students at Pepper Tree Elementary, an ethnically diverse school located thirty-eight miles east of Los Angeles. Black parents were outraged about the school's response to racist Valentine's Day cards addressed to "my favorite cotton picker" and "my favorite monkey." The cards also included crayon drawings of cotton, a monkey, and a person hanging from a tree.

Beyond receiving the racist valentines, Black parents said their children had been called niggers and taunted with monkey sounds at school for over a year. One interracial couple also said that in honor of Black History Month, classmates who are not Black gave backrubs to Black students. Their daughter's classmates said she was eligible for backrubs only half of February since she's only half Black. The Pepper Tree Valentine's Day card incident garnered significant coverage on most local television stations in the Los Angeles metropolitan area, as well as in the *Los Angeles Times*[10] and on CNN.[11] Black parents and others critiqued the principal's mishandling of the situation and deemed her one-page, fairly raceless response letter insufficient.

Pepper Tree's now former principal is not the only leader who failed to meet her school community's expectations amid a highly publicized racial crisis. On a Friday night in August 2017, white nationalists marched through the grounds of the University of Virginia (UVA) carrying lit tiki torches and chanting antisemitic, homophobic, and racist words. That same evening, then-president Teresa A. Sullivan sent a four-sentence statement to the UVA campus community.[12] It said nothing about the "protestors" being white supremacists or anything about racism, antisemitism, or homophobia. Sullivan released a longer statement the following morning that once mentioned "alt-right protestors"—but still no mention of white nationalists or any specifics about what their "intimidating and abhorrent behavior" entailed. In a *Los Angeles Times* article, a colleague and I critiqued the inadequacy of Sullivan's statements.[13] The UVA and Pepper Tree cases are just two examples of what happens when people ascend to leadership roles in K–12 and postsecondary contexts without having learned how to solve racial problems.

Truth 8: The Curriculum Remains Too White

In my campus racial climate research, students of color and their white peers consistently say they learn far too little about non-white communities in college classrooms. Unless one chooses to take a sociology or psychology of race elective or an ethnic studies course, a student could matriculate through four or more years of undergraduate studies without ever engaging content pertaining to America's racial past or present. Throughout the 1990s and 2000s, colleges and universities increasingly introduced diversity requirements into the curriculum. UCLA Professor Mitchell J. Chang's research shows that these requirements produce positive outcomes for students.[14] Notwithstanding their impact, there are at least two noteworthy problems with these mandatory courses. First, because curricular requirement policies usually take years of back-and-forth disagreement among professors and academic senates, watered-down courses that minimally focus on diversity often end up being the compromise. Too few focus deeply on race, racism, and racial equity in the US. The second major problem is the presumption that a single required diversity course will equip students with the literacy and skills they need to live and work in racially complex contexts after college. It does not.

As noted earlier in this chapter, nearly 70 percent of assistant, associate, and full professors are white; the majority of them are white men. Although faculties have slowly diversified over the years, newcomers to the professoriate continue to inherit a curriculum that was mostly fashioned by white men and a smaller number of white women in their academic departments. In my center's professional learning programs, faculty members across racial groups admit that they and their colleagues do not collaborate often enough on ensuring that the curriculum is inclusive of racially, ethnically, and culturally linguistically diverse learners. Instead, academic freedom is typically used as an excuse to let faculty members teach what they want in their courses.

In K–12 contexts, textbooks have become measurably more inclusive over the past few decades.[15] That inclusion is mostly reflected in pictures of diverse peoples and word problems that include ethnic-sounding names and other cultural cues (for example, Saúl shopping at the bodega on his block instead of at Trader Joe's). Despite such intentionality in the textbook publishing industry, educators and students alike tell me that topics that substantively focus on Asian American, Black, Indigenous, and Latino peoples, histories, cultures, and communities remain undertaught. The demographics of the K–12 teaching profession raise reasonable doubts about woke, racially divisive lessons being delivered as alternatives to state-approved textbooks and curricula. How many white women are *actually* doing this, where do they work, and where is the evidence of their harm? As previously noted, many K–12 teachers and administrators across racial and ethnic groups say they did not learn enough about race when they were in college and graduate school. Could it be that someway, somehow, they miraculously figured out how to integrate racial lessons that they themselves never learned into curricula in their schools? It is unlikely or, at best, rare.

Truth 9: Racial Equity Efforts Have Always Been Underfunded

Culture centers and multicultural affairs offices on college campuses have long been disadvantaged by too few staff, inadequate facilities, and insufficient budgets.[16] Likewise, while chief diversity officers (CDOs) have increased in number over the past twenty years, they are almost always given too little money to deliver the level of programming and corrective actions that many predominantly white institutions need. In a recent national survey, nearly a third of CDOs reported that their annual budgets were $39,000 or less.[17] Ethnic studies programs and departments (the academic units where most of the teaching and learning about race and racism occurs on campuses) have been underfunded over the entirety of their existence on lots of campuses.

Florida Governor Ron DeSantis banned the expenditure of taxpayer dollars on DEI offices and programs.[18] SB 17, a bill that Texas Governor Greg Abbott signed into law in June 2023, has done the same.[19] In November 2023, the Associated Press reported the following about DEI cuts at universities in Wisconsin: "The Legislature's budget committee voted in June to eliminate 188 diversity, equity and inclusion positions within the University system and slash UW's budget by $32 million, which is the amount Republicans estimated would be spent on so-called DEI programs over the next two years."[20] Unarguably, $32 million is a significant amount of money. Yet, it is important to note that it is just 0.4 percent of the budget for a thirteen-campus system that annually enrolls approximately 161,000 students and employs more than 35,000 people throughout the state.[21] This is just one example of how little institutions and states invest in DEI initiatives. Relative to other expenditures, spending on these efforts are tiny, which says a lot about how little campus leaders and state legislators value them. At most higher education institutions I visit for research or consulting activities, professionals in culture centers and multicultural affairs offices express tremendous disappointment about their budgets, staff sizes, and inadequate (at times dilapidated) physical spaces. CDOs tell me they need more, not less, money to effectively do their jobs.

Truth 10: CRT Is Barely Taught in Universities

I created and taught a graduate-level course on CRT in 2008. It was the first-ever CRT course taught at the Penn Graduate School of Education. I offered it just about every year thereafter until I transitioned to the University of Southern California in 2017. Students at USC Rossier, a graduate school of education, have eagerly taken the course each year I have taught it here. At neither university did I or anyone else make any student enroll in my CRT course—it always has been and continues to be an elective. Despite this, every year most students generously write, "This course should be required." on my end-of-semester teaching evaluations. I do not believe it was because I somehow indoctrinated or otherwise brainwashed them.

Having taught this course longer than I have any other over my twenty-year faculty career and having used CRT in my own research, I consider myself an expert on the topic. I know what it is (and isn't), where it came from, and what its architects and subsequent academic innovators intended it to do. Harvard Law School Professor Derrick Bell and other legal scholars created CRT for their academic field, the legal profession, and the courts.[22] It is too sophisticated to be taught to elementary and middle school students. I would be surprised, in fact, if high school teachers found some way to introduce CRT to their students—I cannot imagine why or under what circumstances. Also, given the large numbers of undergraduates and graduate student participants in my campus climate studies who tell me they learn too few racial facts and are barely (if at all) exposed to introductory racial concepts in college classrooms, I seriously doubt they are learning the tenets, propositions, and theses that comprise CRT. Who is teaching it to them? At how many colleges and universities? In how many courses? I just searched the online academic catalogues of each of the twenty-five highest-ranked American law schools. Twenty-one offer courses on CRT. I invite anyone to furnish a list of twenty-one K–12 schools across the country where CRT is being taught.

One Very Big Lie

Thousands, perhaps millions of too-woke educators in K–12 schools and postsecondary institutions are indoctrinating students with racist falsehoods about America, teaching homoerotic and otherwise inappropriately pornographic content in classrooms, exposing third graders to CRT, erasing the founding fathers and long-celebrated white American heroes from the curriculum, discarding Shakespeare and other classics in exchange for racially inflammatory texts, forcing kids to pick genders that misalign with who they feel they really are at the time, telling white students they all are racist oppressors, convincing students of color they are all inferior to whites and will be forever oppressed, discriminating against white applicants for everything (university admissions, professorships, presidencies and other high-level administrative jobs, etc.), wasting enormous sums of taxpayers' money on divisive programming, supporting hateful CDOs who aim to embarrass white people and fracture campus communities along racial lines, and grooming young people to hate America because it is so racist. This is one very big, reprehensible, destructive, and politically poisonous lie.

Former US president Donald Trump, several governors and congresspersons, conservative strategists and think tanks, right-wing media outlets, overwhelmingly white groups like Moms for Liberty, politically self-interested and opportunistic school board members, and white supremacists have collaborated to engineer and disseminate this very big lie all across the country. They are succeeding. America is losing. In chapter 12, I forecast some of the long-term damage The Big Lie will do to our democracy, its citizens, its educational institutions, and its workplaces. Here is one additional prediction I will offer now: the ten truths presented in this chapter will become even more true if The Big Lie is not courageously confronted and swiftly discontinued. Educators and everyone else who truly cares about our democracy must boldly defend truths about racial realities in schools and society.

CHAPTER 3

Why Book Bans Are Occurring in Schools and What Is Being Done to Stop Them

John Pascarella III

In his epilogue to *Faces at the Bottom of the Well*, critical race theorist Derrick Bell offers a concluding missive written to his allegorical protagonist, Geneva Crenshaw, a civil rights lawyer with whom he discusses the permanence of racism:

> Perhaps those of us who can admit we are imprisoned by the history of racial subordination in America can accept—as slaves had no choice but to accept—our fate. Not that we legitimate the racism of the oppressor. On the contrary, we can only *de*legitimate it if we can accurately pinpoint it. And racism lies at the center, not the periphery; in the permanent,

> not in the fleeting; in the real lives of black and white people, not in the sentimental caverns of the mind.[1]

Central to the recent surge of book bans in the United States is what Bell described as the permanence of racism, a permanence deeply entrenched and interdependent with homophobia and transphobia. In highly politicized efforts to legitimate policy mechanisms to censor, constrain, or eliminate access to knowledge about racism and sexuality, groups of well-funded conservative thinktanks, politicians, writers, and media figures have stoked widespread fear, resentment, and violence at school board meetings throughout the country by promulgating misinformation about which books are available to whom and which stories or truths can be told in K–12 classrooms.[2]

Forty-four states have advanced legislation, executive orders, and board resolutions since January 2021 to constrain, ban, or criminalize discussions of race, racism, gender diversity, and sexuality.[3] School districts in thirty-two states during the 2021–2022 school year and twenty-one states during the first half of 2022–2023 have introduced 4,003 book bans, targeting books featuring BIPOC (Black, Indigenous, or people of color) and LGBTQIA2S+ (lesbian, gay, bisexual, transgender, questioning, intersex, asexual, or two-spirit) authors and/or characters.[4] News reports of the vilification and termination of K–12 and university educators[5] who have publicly defied "Ed Scare" policies[6] have led many educators and families to leave the districts and states in which these draconian measures have been enforced, while others wonder if they will be the next "political refugees" seeking asylum elsewhere.[7]

How Did We Get Here?

Banning books is an authoritarian tactic to prevent access to knowledge, promote social illiteracy, and legitimize misinformation that maintains preexisting social and political orders. In the US, the maneuver dates back to its founding, during which political pamphlets and books protesting British rule were burned, as were the people or printing houses that produced them. Censorship of literature, art, and music is well documented throughout US history, most notably any works calling for or suggesting the abolishment of slavery or supporting women's suffrage, Indigenous rights, civil rights, Black Power, immigrants' rights, LGBTQIA2S+ rights, the rights of incarcerated people, and/or the rights of individuals and groups otherwise historically marginalized, minoritized, and disenfranchised.[8] This highly politicized strategy follows more than two thousand years of global history, in which countless colonial and imperial leaders banned or burned books deemed controversial, wicked, impure, or contrary to the prevailing political order and then persecuted the authors, scholars, poets, artists, or advocates who created those works.[9] Inevitably, many are punished, but the maneuver eventually fails.

The recent wave of book bans in the US has been characterized as a battle over what K–12 students should learn,[10] brought on by prevailing Western beliefs about childhood innocence and common misapprehensions parents or caregivers might hold regarding youth accessing books deemed not age-appropriate.[11] However, when surveyed, the majority of parents and voters across political affiliations have high confidence in librarians and educators making decisions about which books are available to K–12 students. In 2022, the American Library Association polled 1,000 voters and 472 parents of school-age children, finding that 75 percent of Democrats, 58 percent of Independents, and 70 percent of Republicans opposed book bans; 90 percent of voters and 92 percent of parents reported high regard for librarians, and 75 percent of voters and 80 percent of parents had high confidence in librarians making good decisions about selecting and offering books in their collections.[12] A recent investigation by *The Washington Post* that analyzed school district records throughout the country found that the vast majority of book challenges originated from individuals who were serial (60 percent, ten or more times) or repeat (25 percent%, two to nine times) filers.[13] As more evidence becomes available, it has become clearer that the battle over book bans is not being waged by droves of outraged parents.

In her recent *Education Week* op-ed, Columbia University professor Bettina L. Love described the false narrative conservative groups and leaders are invoking about K–12 schools, labeling them "woke" for political gain. She asks, "Where are all the "woke" books?" The truth, she points out, is that schools are not inundated with books about racism or sexuality:

> Our schools are labeled "woke" when students encounter books that discuss race and racism, among other topics now deemed inappropriate. But where are all these books? From 2020 to 2021, only a little more than 12 percent of the books that made the children's bestsellers list were about Black or African characters. And fewer than 8 percent of bestselling

books were written by Black or African authors. These numbers mean the average public school library is overwhelmingly filled with books by and about white people. By the way Republicans tell it, our school libraries are liberal havens for books centered on race that feed the woke movement supposedly taking over our schools.[14]

Decades of research demonstrate that race, gender, and sexuality are not centered in most K–12 curricula in the US,[15] nor are these topics prominently featured in the majority of books K–12 students can readily access in their school libraries,[16] nor are these subjects present in the bulk of coursework most college students will ever encounter while obtaining a degree, despite evidence that coursework centering on racial and sexual diversity benefits all students.[17]

In 2020, just one year before conservative states and school districts sharply increased book bans and began placing countless restrictions on diversity, equity, and inclusion (DEI) initiatives, scholars Shilpi Sinha and Shaireen Rasheed published a study describing the resurgence of racial tensions by white students in university classrooms, noting the historical juncture that had occurred under the Trump administration: "The United States is currently seeing a resurgence of white nationalist sentiment, an exacerbation of racial divisions and tensions, an uptick in hate crimes, and bullying increasingly targeting immigrant youth, all of which, in the current political and cultural climate have often been legitimized through a recourse to 'alternative facts.'"[18] Pulitzer Prize-winning journalist Wesley Lowery described this resurgence as a "whitelash" to the "browning of America," spurred by far-right politicians and news media figures, brought on by growing fear among white people about the nation's changing racial demographics.[19] In his recent book, *American Whitelash*, Lowery notes:

> For most of American history, white supremacy has been a dispositionally conservative ideology aiming to preserve a racial caste system in which white Americans were the only true citizens. Yet the advent of multiracial democracy through the Second Reconstruction and the perceived browning of America through immigration has forced today's white supremacists to accept as a premise that they're "losing." No longer can they claim, as their forebears did, that they aim to return to the norm of white supremacists status quo. Today's white supremacist movement is revolutionary—its explicit aim being to overthrow our maturing multiracial democracy.[20]

Lowery, as well as education researchers Francesca López and Christine Sleeter, differentiate present-day conservative attacks on education from those espoused in the 1990s and early 2000s targeting multicultural education. Predominately white conservative critics then charged culturally relevant curricula as "intellectually weak, consisting of a smattering of politically correct trivia and dogma that replaced sound intellectual scholarship with shoddiness, and objective fact with subjective sentiment."[21] Although these decades-old arguments are strikingly similar to recent condemnation of teaching or reading books about racism and sexuality in K–12 schools, today's attacks are led by several conservative governors, state legislators, and school board presidents signing gag orders, banning books, and sanctioning or firing teachers and administrators who refuse to comply with censorship mandates.

How Are Stakeholders Fighting Back?

As conservative lawmakers and school board members continue to propose legislation and resolutions prohibiting books, curricula, or other learning materials that address concepts including racism and sexuality, local and state coalitions of educators, community members, and students have organized to defeat these measures. Numerous nonprofit organizations and companies are supporting these coalitions, including PEN America, the National Education Association (NEA), the Human Rights Campaign (HRC), the Southern Poverty Law Center (SPLC), and the American Civil Liberties Union (ACLU). The examples shared in this section illustrate the strategies, resources, and legal action stakeholders are deploying to fight back against book bans and censorship measures in favor of teaching the truth about racism, homophobia, and transphobia in schools.

PEN America, a nationwide network of writers, poets, playwrights, journalists, publishers, and other writing professionals,[22] carefully tracks individual book bans reported in local public schools and libraries across the US, actively campaigns against educational gag orders, organizes advocacy events and festivals, promotes campus free speech policies, frequently generates comprehensive reports on bans and censorship, and produces several advocacy resources. In partnership with Penguin Random House, PEN America recently filed a federal lawsuit challenging book removals from Escambia County schools in Florida.[23] Penguin Random House has also joined lawsuits with the Association of American Publishers challenging Texas HB 900 and Arkansas Act 372, both of which ban books based on content and viewpoint in libraries, schools, and businesses.[24]

The NEA has produced and disseminated "Know Your Rights" guides, board resolution samples, and letter templates to support teachers teaching in states or districts banning books or restricting how racism and sexuality can be taught.[25] In June 2023, the HRC declared a state of emergency for LGBTQIA2+ people in the US and released an LGBTQ+ guidebook for action that provides a state-by-state rundown of anti-LGBTQ+ policies and resources for filing complaints, engaging in local advocacy, and navigating board meetings and conversations with friends and families. The SPLC actively tracks active hate groups and extremists, reports their activities to law enforcement and news media, and files lawsuits defending victims of discrimination and hate. SPLC's educational program, Learning for Justice, regularly produces and disseminates instructional plans, activist toolkits, and professional learning opportunities for educators to teach truthful, age-appropriate lessons on racism, sexism, antisemitism, Islamophobia, xenophobia, homophobia, transphobia, and other discriminatory ideologies. The ACLU has also filed multiple lawsuits opposing gag order legislation in various states, including Oklahoma, Texas, Florida, and New Hampshire.[26]

What More Can We Do?

While book bans and gag orders vary widely and have been enforced differently in each state or local district, far-right conservatives advocating these measures consistently rely on three key tactics: sharing personal anecdotes that presume a white perspective; cherry-picking, decontextualizing, and evangelizing incomplete examples; and proselytizing misinformation as evidence-based theories. News media and social media tools have powerfully amplified these messages to create what López and Sleeter call propaganda ecosystems, "designed to incite anger and mislead the public into believing that far Right solutions will assuage their concerns."[27] In this final section, three practical strategies for advocating against book bans are presented to assist educators and stakeholders in K–12 schools, colleges, and universities.

- **Truthful Relationships: Build Meaningful Connections, Seek Honest Perspectives.** Educators who spend time in their school communities meaningfully connecting with parents, caregivers, and other community stakeholders to learn their honest perspectives on book bans and the individuals asserting them are more likely to garner support and build coalitions that disrupt censorship efforts on their campuses. Connecting with book ban advocates outside of high stakes meetings has the potential to deescalate opposition, clear up misinformation, and increase truthful, transparent conversations. In some cases, educators have learned that book ban filers are not parents or caregivers of students in the district or community, have not read the books being targeted, and do not know much about the curriculum or program in which the book might be used or accessed. In other instances, educators have learned that a book ban advocate is a beloved and respected community leader who has brought a group of supporters with them. Taking the time to connect, listen, and personally engage fellow community members is necessary for disrupting book bans and censorship measures with community input and backing, especially when the community is divided in supporting those initiatives.[28]

- **Truthful Evidence: Work Together, Gather Robust Data.** Educators can work together to systematically review books, curriculum, and coursework materials to more accurately account for the representation of race, gender, and sexuality in their schools or departments. Doing so can (1) reveal hidden patterns of inequity in the inclusion of BIPOC and LGBTQIA2+ authors, experts, artists, and historical figures; (2) raise awareness about the persistence of exclusionary practices; and (3) alter the ways data are discussed by presenting concrete evidence of those disparities. Educational researchers can partner with community stakeholders to survey local parents, caregivers, and students on their true perceptions of book bans or censorship measures affecting which books and content can be taught at their schools. Most importantly, carefully read the whole book being challenged—not just the decontextualized passages or images targeted. Doing so can reveal the whole story, the integrity of the themes and characters, and the credibility of the authors being attacked. Gathering, interpreting, and reporting multiple data points can shift the focus of what constitutes valid and reliable evidence guiding decisions about policies, resolutions, or other decisions that undermine educational equity.
- **Truthful Messaging: Provide Clear, Consistent, and Evidence-Based Messaging.** The freedom to access and read books featuring BIPOC and LGBTQIA2+ authors and characters, including subject matter that centers on race, gender, sexuality, ethnicity, culture, language, and identity, is a constitutionally protected right that has

been repeatedly upheld by the Supreme Court. Educators can consistently stay on message when interacting with book ban advocates by being clear about the state content standards that guide their planning decisions to ensure accurate, complete, and deliberate inclusion of diverse identities, voices, and histories in their selection of books and curriculum materials. Parents retain the right to access and evaluate the content being taught, including the books their children access in public schools. When a parent or student challenges a book or lesson being taught, the school or department should offer a legally permissible review process that takes the concern seriously and evaluates the merits of the complaint. The Association for Supervision and Curriculum Development (ASCD) and the National Coalition Against Censorship generated book review protocols that offer educators and community stakeholders practical guidelines.[29] Introducing and sustaining a formal review process enables educators to respond to complaints with a clear, consistent, and evidence-based message and enables complainants to be taken seriously.

Conclusion

Despite conservative theories espousing misinformation that learning about the history of racism, homophobia, and transphobia is divisive and unpatriotic, banning books is quintessentially anti-American. The maneuver flies in the face of the First Amendment to the US Constitution and has repeatedly failed throughout history, despite painstaking efforts to suppress the voices and views of marginalized and excluded people living in America. Although far-right conservatives continue to advance and pass vaguely worded censorship measures and book bans, Derrick Bell reminds us:

> Armed with knowledge, and with the enlightened, humility-based commitment that engenders, we can accept the dilemmas of committed confrontation with evils we cannot end. We can go forth to serve, knowing that our failure to act will not change conditions and may very well worsen them. We can listen to those who have been most subordinated. In listening, we must not do them the injustice of failing to recognize that somehow they survived as complete, defiant, though horribly scarred beings. We must learn from their example, learn from those whom we would teach.[30]

The struggle for equal access to educational opportunity in the US has made only incremental progress, has not been inevitable, and has endured many setbacks. Educators in K–12 schools, colleges, and universities must remain committed to their vital role in preparing young people to access and learn the accurate history of racism, homophobia, and transphobia. In doing so, educators must humanize themselves, their students, and their critics in the greater effort to increase equity and justice for all.

CHAPTER 4

Raising Our Consciousness

Teachers as Leaders for Racial Equity

Erica S. Silva

Teaching in today's political climate requires all of us, as educators, to reexamine our beliefs, classroom practices, and how we engage with our community during a time of deep politicization of K–12 education. As a former teacher and instructional coach, and now as a teacher educator, I have reflected on the political environment we now find ourselves in as a country and within our profession. What I know is this: teaching is hard. Teaching in our current polarized educational context is even harder. Many educators say that teaching postpandemic is arguably the hardest time in their educational careers. Teachers, principals, librarians, counselors, school board members, and other school and district leaders are confronting one of the most deeply divided times in education since school integration in the 1960s.

Despite years of progress to build more equitable schooling environments, our country's deep polarization has led to attacks on teaching and learning in K–12 schools across the country. To date, 32 states have book bans in place, and 223 anti-critical race theory (CRT) measures have been enacted in K–12 schools across the country with—a whopping 91 percent of anti-CRT measures being targeted at K–12 education[1]. Consequently, educators today must understand the new political climate that the National Education Association (NEA) calls "Teaching in an Era of Polarization."[2] Many teachers are actively seeking support to better understand the political climate they are teaching in and how to best serve their students during a time of censorship, book bans, and the politicization of K–12 classrooms.

This chapter focuses on what educators can do during a time when school boards and state legislators are implementing restrictive policies pertaining to teaching about America's racial past and present. I challenge our profession to critically examine these three areas: (1) examining the truth within ourselves, (2) examining the truth within our classrooms, and (3) organizing for the truth in our communities. As a classroom teacher, I often found myself frequently frustrated by the mandates, board agendas, and instructional priorities set by someone outside of the classroom space. I often felt powerless in the decision-making that was happening around me, but not with me, about the space that I was charged with (my classroom). Over time, I began to critically think about and analyze the way policies and practices are passed and implemented at the school board or district level and how they impacted the classroom. As I moved through my career and examined this from the classroom, the district, and now through the lens of teacher preparation, I look back on my K–12 classroom experience and realize I had more agency and power than I felt at the time. As a result, I present three lenses of opportunity for educators to reexamine their agency during this politically volatile chapter in our nation's history, which may otherwise result in a generation of children harmed by restrictive and oppressive educational policies across the country.

Examining the Truth Within Ourselves

Paolo Freire reminds us that "The educator has the duty of not being neutral."[3] Every decision we make in the classroom is not a neutral one. The decision to include or exclude a novel, swap out one activity for another, or skip a lesson are all influenced by lived experiences, fears, beliefs, thoughts, biases, and prior knowledge. As we navigate the current political environment, we must turn inward and critically analyze and reflect on the role we play in either perpetuating inequities or dismantling them within ourselves and our classrooms.

Meaningful truth begins with us. It requires critical self-reflection, what Sealey-Ruiz deems engaging in an "archeology of self."[4] To critically analyze and question oppressive policies and practices being introduced in our communities, educators must have a deep understanding of their beliefs, assumptions, and biases. Sealey-Ruiz discusses the importance of how starting with the "self" empowers educators to build their own racial literacy and political/social consciousness. Cherry-Paul argues that teachers need to raise the level of their own critical consciousness in schools.[5] Critical consciousness in educators focuses on developing their ability to examine oppressive beliefs, along with unjust classroom practices and school policies. Teachers are not only responsible for raising the critical consciousness of their students, but we must also raise our own level of critical consciousness, particularly at a time when conservative right-wing curriculums are being approved for use in Florida, librarians are being required to complete compliance reports for legislators in North Dakota, and school boards reject the state-adopted social studies curriculum in California[6]. Failing to do the necessary "self" work required of building our own racial literacy hinders the development of the critical lens necessary to examine problematic curriculum, policies, and practices when they are enacted in our communities.

Engage in Race-Conscious Professional Learning

Teachers who examine the truth within themselves raise their level of critical consciousness by engaging in race-conscious professional learning. I encourage educators to participate in race-conscious professional development (PD) opportunities. In states that have explicitly banned this type of learning, educators are encouraged to seek out their own professional learning by engaging in free webinars by educational advocacy organizations such as Learning for Justice. This type of PD will enable us all to understand how race-neutral ideologies are pervasive within the field and begin to empower ourselves to validate the racial, linguistic, and cultural backgrounds of our students. Choosing to actively engage in equity-minded PD provides us with an opportunity to engage in important unlearning and see our classroom practice and curriculum with a critical lens. In addition, abandoning long-held race-neutral beliefs that are pervasive in the K–12 space enables us to acknowledge the racialized experiences of our students and makes us better educators. Statements such as, "I don't see color" or "I treat all my students the same," fail to acknowledge how the way we teach and show up in our classroom is informed by both our explicit and implicit biases, beliefs, perceptions, and lived experiences, particularly those around race. By engaging in race-conscious professional learning, we better equip ourselves to build more equitable classroom environments.

Abandon Race-Neutral Beliefs and Dismantle Internalized Whiteness

Furthermore, I challenge all of us as educators to not only work to abandon race-neutral beliefs, but to engage in the unlearning necessary to dismantle internalized whiteness and white supremacy within ourselves. This practice is often deeply personal and painful, due to the fact that for many educators of color, in particular those who come from immigrant backgrounds, assimilation and survival in this country is rooted in proximity to whiteness. Furthermore, educators of color who found success in academia/education often unknowingly perpetuate aptitudes that include "Well if I did it, you should do it too" without questioning why other students of color should have to survive in the same environments that were hostile to us as educators. Actively working to understand how race-neutral thinking and beliefs work empowers educators to better examine the truth within ourselves and, ultimately, our classroom practices.

Examining the Truth Within Our Classrooms

Educators who engage in critical self-reflection and their own racial literacy development are better equipped to seek "truth" within their classrooms. Seeking truth in our classrooms means that we see, validate, and build classroom environments that are supportive and inclusive of every student, from every background. These classrooms invite student input, empower students with multiple perspectives through critical thinking and problem solving, and center equity in their policies and practices. As a result, students learn in environments where their identities are honored and lived experiences are centered and where they can think critically about the world around them.

Teachers who examine truth within their classrooms *understand the true origins of CRT and how conservatives have weaponized a long-held legal theory by falsely claiming it is taught in K–12 schools.* One of the biggest challenges I have noted in my journey from being a K–12 teacher to higher education is the chasm between theory, scholarship, and practice. To mitigate this, I believe it is important for schools and districts to provide teachers with a deeper understanding of the critical components of culturally responsive pedagogy to enable them to distinguish it from CRT and the accusations that come along with it. Empowering teachers with access to culturally responsive pedagogy research, and not secondhand summaries, places teachers to be in the position of both a learner and an expert.

There is a wealth of misinformation surrounding the idea that CRT is directly being taught to students in K–12 schools. I posit that the majority of the nation's teachers did not learn about CRT in their teacher preparation programs. Therefore, it is essential that educators understand what CRT is and is not in order to better prepare ourselves for when we are questioned by a parent, community member, administrator, or school board member on the use of CRT in classrooms. In an era filled with misinformation, distorted perceptions, and agenda-riddled platforms, we can better prepare ourselves as educators and, by doing so, feel more secure in our instructional decision-making.

Critically Consume Curriculum

Teachers must also be critical consumers of information and knowledge. In addition to teaching our students how to be critical consumers of information, we must also critically consume the curriculum and textbooks provided to us. For example, a teacher interested in implementing ethnic studies in their classroom might Google ethnic studies resources. I engaged in this search and stumbled across a website at the top of my Google search with a site that spoke to quality curriculum and an emphasis on equality—which at face value, looked legitimate. After further digging, I began to see clues that indicated this was sponsored by an antiequity organization working against race-consciousness in ethnic studies.

When materials are placed in front of us as teachers, it is our duty and responsibility to critically examine curriculum to ensure that it is culturally responsive and sustaining. Educators who work in restrictive curricular environments can embed critical questions in their direct instruction to empower students to seek the truth on topics by structuring questions to have students thinking about multiple perspectives of characters, historical figures, and topics—with an emphasis on the difference between facts and opinions. Some questions educators might ask as they evaluate texts include the following: What books/texts do I look forward to teaching my students every year? What is it about these texts that makes them something that I enjoy and look forward to? Have I read this text with a critically conscious lens and evaluated if this text is culturally responsive compared to the traditional cannon? If we read a text from the traditional cannon, how can we use questioning to push student thinking to examine multiple perspectives?

Focus on Evidence-Based Critical Thinking

Classroom instruction is always grounded in standards. Every year, teachers work in a community with one another to assess their students and build curricular plans for the school year. Prioritizing teaching the truth about America's racial past and present means anchoring this work in evidence-based critical thinking standards outlined in the Common Core. Building units focused on the Common Core anchor standards, such as the "integration of knowledge and ideas," "research to build and present knowledge," "comprehension and collaboration," provides the instructional foundation to build student's critical thinking skills across texts and subject matter.

Even in districts where books are being banned, teachers can engage with texts by asking students questions such as How is the character represented? Which characters are given voice? Which characters are silenced? What stereotypes or tropes are present? How does the author use language to represent this character? This develops students' thinking, regardless of what text is in front of them. In addition, teaching students how to utilize textual evidence and identify the difference between facts and opinions raises their own critical consciousness as they begin to analyze the world around them.

Examine Long-Held Classroom Practices and Beliefs by Engaging in Racial Noticing, as Defined by Shah and Coles

While states may attempt to ban book titles and other instructional materials, they cannot censor the ways in which we treat students more equitably. As policy makers make efforts to censor the books in teachers' classroom libraries and what teachers can say in schools, teachers can alternatively begin to focus on their own pedagogical practices, despite what the law may allow on their shelves. This looks like what Shah and Coles call "racial noticing" in the K–12 classroom.[7] Teachers who engage in racial noticing attend to, interpret, and respond to racial phenomena in their classrooms. Understanding and engaging in racial noticing in the classroom allows us to see the way that race becomes salient in our classroom, through student interactions along with how it emerges in our own classroom policies, practices, and interactions with students. Engaging in racial noticing in our classroom provides us with a starting point on how we can work to address racial inequities in schools. By doing so, we turn our attention to our actions as educators when focusing on advancing racial equity in schools.

Organizing for the Truth in Our Communities

Now more than ever it is important for teachers to not do the work of advancing equity in isolation, but to find and draw strength from like-minded educators who are also committed to racial justice in schools. Actively seeking out these spaces throughout my career has sustained me when burnout is real, stress is high, and the work seems insurmountable. The encouragement and support of my colleagues across the country fills my cup—and I encourage every educator to do the same.

Teachers who organize for truth in our communities *engage in educational advocacy by seeking out the support of like-minded colleagues beyond their workplaces.* Seeking out the support of like-minded colleagues, particularly when working in highly contentious districts, provides educators with emotional support as they learn how to navigate restrictive laws and policies together. The support of nonprofit advocacy groups unaffiliated with one's employer allows us to share our experiences in a nonjudgmental, supportive environment. Building these spaces is critical in supporting teachers, and educators of color in particular, when their livelihoods and very existence are threatened.

Teachers can also amplify their lived experiences inside and outside the classroom by participating in advocacy campaigns, writing op-eds, and presenting at educational conferences and other media initiatives to better educate the public, from the teacher's perspective, about the long-lasting and dangerous effects of book bans and policies aimed at quelling equity initiatives. Teachers who work to stay informed and make connections in the policy and advocacy space will be better prepared to combat opposition they may face in their classrooms and school communities. Working in the community with nonprofit advocacy groups and teachers has the potential to build grassroots movements in communities facing censorship, book bans, and other far-right protests.

Increase Their Level of Civic Engagement and Participation in Local School Board Races

Beyond advocacy, we must encourage and support more educators to run for school board or be involved in local school board elections. Putting forth more school board candidates who are not only racially diverse, but who intimately understand the teaching profession can powerfully shape board agendas, priorities, policies, and superintendent selection. I have witnessed the power of grassroot teacher candidates being elected to their community's school board (note: teachers are unable to run for a seat in the district they work in). In fact, many board races have uncontested seats, providing highly organized candidates an opportunity to run and win successful campaigns.[8] With powerful organizations such as a teacher's union behind them, teacher school board candidates are a viable, underrepresented, and underutilized strategy in fighting the conservative assault on school boards.

Centering the Truth

Teaching with racial equity at the center of our practice requires truth-telling. It requires us to be honest with ourselves and our biases. It requires us to critically examine our long-held classroom traditions, pedagogy, beloved books, and classroom practices. It requires community—partnering across grade levels, schools, districts, and communities. It requires us to reach beyond our comfort zones and organize with like-minded educators, inside and outside our school communities. The truth about teaching in a politically divisive and dangerous time is that the work of advancing racial justice and equity cannot be done in isolation. The challenge for today's classroom teachers and educators across our country is to recognize the inherent power we have to directly impact and change the lives of the students we teach in our classrooms. We must equip those of us committed to the truth about our country's past and present with the information, tools, support, and resources to sustain ourselves when our livelihood and practice may be challenged.

For administrators and educational leaders supporting teachers, I encourage you to reflect on how teachers are supported during this time with the following questions:

- Are there opportunities on my campus for race-conscious learning? In what ways do I support teachers who are willing to participate in PD or conferences outside our district? Do I, as an administrator, actively participate in race-conscious leadership PD?
- How do I actively disrupt race-neutral beliefs and language on my campus?
- How does our school map out intentional time for teacher collaboration and culturally responsive curriculum development?
- How can I, as a school leader, engage in "racial noticing" on my campus?
- Do I provide substitute support for teachers who are interested in participating in educational advocacy opportunities?
- What can I do as a school leader to encourage and develop the civic participation of my school community?

This chapter focuses and unfairly places the burden of truth-telling on America's teachers. Yet, in spite of this,

I believe teachers are the most powerful force to counter the current era of misinformation and polarization. Administrators, parents, and community members must rally around our teachers to give them the support they most desperately need, now more than ever, if we are to educate a generation of students who embrace racial equity and can move our country out of this dark chapter in American history.

CHAPTER 5

Countermeasures to Education Gag Orders

What K–12 Education Leaders Can Do

Francesca López, Ashley Burns Nascimiento,
and Elisa Serrano

In this chapter, we provide readers with an overview of the recent (and ongoing) controversies surrounding education gag orders in K–12 schools. Our aim is to contextualize the rationales and methods behind the efforts, as well as to provide evidence-based recommendations to counter the misinformation efforts. Conservative-led education gag orders and intentional misinformation about equitable education approaches have fueled polarization,[1] disrupted schooling, and incited threats against educators.[2] In many states, education gag orders are eradicating equitable educational approaches due to scholars' and the Supreme Court's interpretation that K–12 teachers do not have academic freedom.[3] This context has created unsafe environments for youth who feel "their very existence is being rejected."[4]

Against the backdrop of a polarized climate, many teachers report a lack of guidance and support from leaders. The most salient of their concerns are parental backlash in social media that can "ruin a teacher's reputation in a single post."[5] Teachers overwhelmingly expressed a need for leader-endorsed resources that provide guidance. However, as reported by Rogers et al., "Rather than providing professional development or other supports to help teachers respond in this challenging context, many [leaders] instead tried to avoid the issue."[6] As a result, many teachers are abandoning equity-focused strategies or leaving the profession altogether.[7] The crisis is most salient for educators of color, which has pronounced implications for high-poverty communities.[8]

Amid these challenges, recent data highlight that a vast majority of parents support inclusive education and report that their top concern is "politicians making decisions about what their children learn in the classroom."[9] This points to an important opportunity for school leaders to mitigate the political polarization in schools by explaining the "what and why of teaching related to controversial topics" and supporting teachers with resources. There is nuance needed, however, given that many explanations provided after misinformation has been spread are largely ineffective.[10] To that end, in this chapter, we present background to the nature of false narratives as well as the extent to which they have been magnified by traditional and social media. We then provide evidence-based recommendations for leaders to counter the spread of misinformation and mitigate polarization, as well as to support teachers in engaging in equity practices.

The Genesis of Education Gag Orders

Although education gag orders and the corresponding book bans may seem recent, the country finds itself in the midst of a manufactured controversy that has been in the making for years.[11] In large part, the current landscape is the result of the exploitation of human emotions by politicians who instill fear in the public and purport to provide a remedy to the often manufactured threat.[12] The sources of the ideas promulgated by conservative politicians can be traced to a network of conservative think tanks that emerged in the 1950s,[13] grew exponentially in the 1970s, and are a present-day international conglomerate with a "mission to champion, spread, defend, and entrench, as widely and deeply as possible and in a multiplicity of contexts" free market ideologies.[14] Before their targets were discussions and curricular materials that focus on race and gender, think tanks contributed to the manufactured crisis in schools that could only be solved with reforms that involved high-stakes testing, choice via charter schools and vouchers, and a myriad of other issues that all seemed to have privatization as the solution.[15] There is a longer history of claims that teachers were indoctrinating students to become socialists.[16]

Conservative think tanks often circumvent peer review to circulate ideas and ideologies (under the guise of research) rapidly, readily, and prolifically.[17] Due to budget cuts to the Congressional Research Service in the late 1970s, the lost capacity was replaced by think tanks,[18] which positioned them as the direct source of ideas and recommendations to conservative politicians. In today's controversies, this is evident in the similar, and sometimes even identical, language from conservative think tank recommendations[19] that can be identified in education gag orders across forty-one states.[20] Although think tanks are prohibited from "exerting direct political influence through lobbying, funding grassroots organizations, or endorsing candidates and legislation"[21] due to their 501(c)(3) status, they circumvent this prohibition by relying on media, facilitated by think tank media relations departments. The media has enhanced the expediency in the transmission of recommendations by think tanks, which extends quickly and broadly to the public.

Both traditional and social media played a substantial role in scaling the false narrative, creating real dilemmas for educators. In an analysis of media coverage focused on "critical race theory" in K–12 schools that spanned September 1, 2020, through August 31, 2021, 53 percent of the stories were covered by conservative outlets (e.g., Fox News). That reflects more than six times the coverage by outlets considered liberal.[22] The coverage was also strategically focused on contexts that were particularly important for elections. As explained by Pollock et al.:

> Districts experiencing the most rapid demographic change (in which the percentage of White student enrollment fell by more than 18% since 2000) were more than three times as likely as districts with minimal or no change in the enrollment of White students to be impacted by the localized conflict campaign. . . . Districts impacted by local campaigns are most likely to enroll a racially mixed and majority White student body and to be located in communities that are politically contested or leaning liberal or conservative, rather

than in communities that voted strongly against or in favor of Trump in the 2020 presidential election.[23]

Thus, fear-inducing campaigns were focused most ardently in contested election contexts. There, the campaigns were not only inducing fear but also providing favorable portrayals of conservative politicians who are campaigning on platforms that oppose "state sanctioned racism" and "collective guilt."[24]

Strategic Manufacturing of an Education Controversy

On a September 2, 2020, episode of *Tucker Carlson Tonight*, Christofer Rufo, a far-right activist funded by conservative think tanks over the years, was featured as a guest. Rufo deliberately sensationalized Critical Race Theory as an "existential threat to the United States," and explicitly urged then-President Trump to issue an executive order to abolish the academic framework from the federal government and to "stamp out this destructive, divisive, pseudoscientific ideology."[25]

The next day, as told to the *New Yorker*, the guest received a call from the White House, confirming that the president was compelled by the episode and urged staff to take immediate action.[26] By September 28, the ultraconservative activist was in Washington D.C. helping draft a related executive order. This was the catalyst to the fears among parents, school board outrage, and educator condemnation. This emerging narrative drove the division that continues to plague many communities across the country today. Driven by unsubstantiated claims and unchecked information, this false narrative slowly—then exponentially—gained momentum across traditional and social media.

Not long after the September 28 executive order banning "any form of race or sex stereotyping or scapegoating," another executive order was issued establishing the President's Advisory 1776 Commission, referred to as the 1776 Project. This commission was an advisory committee established by former President Donald Trump to support what he called "patriotic education." The commission, which included no historians specializing in United States history, released the 1776 Report on January 18, 2021, two days before the end of the forty-fifth presidential term.

From the analysis of eighteen months of media coverage about public education funding in June 2021, the pervasiveness of this false narrative became clear both in qualitative focus groups and quantitative analysis. Within state-specific analyses and a national media analysis, an unexpected pattern emerged, and the previously nascent term "critical race theory" (CRT) was surfacing across the country. With deeper digging, the data revealed a manufactured controversy and growing division exacerbated by traditional and social media.

The Proliferation of a Recurring News Cycle

NetBase Quid is an artificial intelligence platform capable of accessing over one billion articles from more than 3.6 million global news and blog sources. Our Quid search for articles containing "critical race theory" and "education" between December 31, 2019, and June 23, 2021, resulted in over 2,400 unique articles. As shown in table 5.1, the top cluster (the largest category of stories with similar language and topics) is framed as defining "what CRT really is," followed by political and legislative activities in Florida. Eleven of the top fifteen clusters were explicitly focused on so-called anti-CRT legisla-

Table 5.1 Top 20 clusters from QUID network map

Topic	News stories	
	n	%
What CRT really is	341	13.8
Florida and Ron DeSantis legislation	246	10.0
School district-level coverage	217	8.8
Anti-CRT	170	6.9
Idaho legislation	167	6.8
"Dangers" of CRT	140	5.7
CRT curriculum in classrooms	122	5.0
Texas legislation	115	4.7
Biden DOE equity efforts	115	4.7
Virginia debate	111	4.5
Congressional CRT legislation	102	4.1
Critical race theory bans	102	4.1
Georgia debate	99	4.0
Efforts to block CRT and equity funding	91	3.7
Trump executive order	86	3.5
Oklahoma legislation	71	2.9
Utah legislation	66	2.7
Tennessee debate	52	2.1
Trump 1776 Commission	51	2.1

Note: Quid is an artificial intelligence platform capable of accessing over 1 billion articles from more than 3.6 million global news and blog sources. With this network map, or search query, these "clusters" have the largest volume of stories and are grouped together based on language and topical similarities.

tion. The latter is notable because none of this was actually about the legal framework CRT; hence, calling the legislation anti-CRT is neither factual nor neutral.

As indicated in figure 5.1, there was a noticeable absence of media coverage discussing any topic positioned as "critical race theory" prior to September 2020. However, the timeline shows a slight uptick in coverage in September due to the 1776 Commission announcement. Naturally, coverage decreased during the presidential election, the transfer of power, and

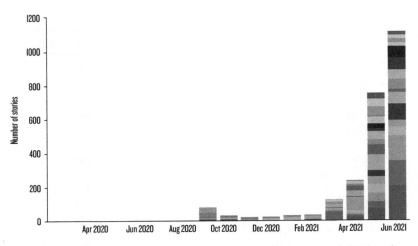

Figure 5.1 News coverage of critical race theory between April 2020 and June 2021

the January 2021 insurrection. As the shock of the insurrection and the frailty of American democracy sunk in, coverage started to surge exponentially in March 2021, particularly as various states introduced similar legislation and implemented education gag orders and antiequity bans. By July of 2021, thousands of articles were available online that would surface in any Google search, including some articles which were shared thousands of times on Facebook. This timeline of events highlights the manufactured nature of the backlash, illustrating a deliberate effort to distort the narrative and generate opposition to inclusive public education.

As mid-2021 became late 2021, the debate and tone for the 2022 midterm elections—even local school board elections—were shaped by a combination of early negative sentiment, misinformation, and manufactured fear. Moreover, the coverage about "what CRT really is" lacked neutrality. The dominating

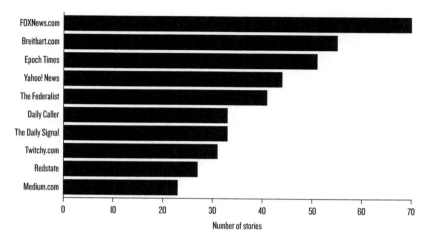

Figure 5.2 Media outlets with the most CRT-related stories

outlets shaping this discourse, with their high publication frequency, consist primarily of far-right, extremist, and ultraconservative media outlets such as Breitbart, Epoch Times, Fox News, and the Federalist (see figure 5.2). Additionally, Fox News not only airs broadcast segments, but also repurposes them across platforms, including online news stories. The Quid search revealed Fox News as the leading outlet, with the highest number of published articles. Its mentions of CRT increased from 3 in June 2020 to 901 in June 2021.

How Education Leaders Can Mitigate Polarization Efforts

While educators and students have personally and professionally suffered from the passage of laws, disinformation, and the chilling effect, education leaders are in particularly influential positions to help bring about meaningful change to the manufactured crises. In part, this is due to the fact that an overwhelming majority (84 percent) of the public trust educators to make decisions about what should be taught regardless of political affiliation.[27] The public also considers access to a full accounting of history, as well as teacher pay and retention, to be among the most serious issues facing schools.[28] In contrast, the vast majority of the public does not consider parental say in book selections and negative aspects of history being taught as issues that are important. As such, the task at hand is not garnering support but demonstrating "that something can be done about the issue."[29] Moreover, transparency between district leaders, educators, and parents is vital in denouncing the misinformation that creates fear and opposition.[30] Taking these factors together, education leaders are in unique positions to diminish waves of dissent that do not represent most families.

Scholars across disciplines have provided crucial knowledge that can contribute to dismantling manufactured fear and false narratives. Among the most robust and recent evidence on countering misinformation is that the efforts must (1) avoid simple denials and, instead, be evidence-based and detailed, (2) reduce polarization, and (3) increase exposure to the topics.[31] Although the first recommendation is straightforward, it is often difficult for school leaders to access summaries of evidence that support the kind of educational equity practices needed in schools. To address the issue, The Aspen Institute released a brief[32] that provides summaries of evidence for use by school leaders and the public. The brief is relatively short and freely accessible, as is the information on the background to the creation of the brief.[33] An important framing of the research when providing details in prioritizing the benefits of equitable education approaches (using terminology that makes sense for the particular context—a point we expand on in the next section) is that all youth benefit from these approaches. Providing explicit examples of pedagogical approaches, lessons, and other means of making the abstract more visible have been effective.[34]

To reduce polarization, evidence points to the importance of refraining from language that incites emotional reactions. Both denouncing individuals as "racist" or avoiding the topic of equity create situations that increase polarization. Polarization has also been identified with terms like "injustices."[35] To reduce polarization, messaging must acknowledge race and racism—not avoid it—as it also establishes the shared stake of education that unites all families across social, economic, and racial differences.[36] Language use is key. Also necessary in reducing polarization is message framing that unites and centers the issue about pedagogy (not politics). In a messaging study made up of participants from varied political, race/ethnic, gender, and age demographics, the following frame received the most support for antiracist education: "The education system in America is outdated, and so is our curriculum about race. We live in a diverse, multiracial country, but our education system hasn't kept up. We need to create a curriculum that accurately and honestly teaches students about race in America to prepare them for the future."[37] It is important to keep in mind that, as mentioned earlier, most families support equitable education approaches, and as such, reducing polarization is as much about affirming positions for allies as it is about quelling controversies. In their report, *Advancing Anti-Racist Education: How School Leaders Can Navigate the Moral Panic about Critical Race Theory*, Sweetland, Pineau, and O'Neil note, "When facing vocal opponents with strident views, remember that your audience is not the immovable opponent, but the quiet supporters, the undecided, and people who have not yet been engaged in the conversation. Your stance should remind the quiet supporters that it is possible to speak up without engaging in vitriol. It should also show the undecided that you are the more reasonable party in the discussion."[38]

To increase exposure requires that the topic of education equity not be reserved for moments when controversies require engaging in the topic but become part of the fabric of conversations in all educational endeavors.[39] As an entry point, an effective strategy has included "expanding people's mental models of racism."[40]

Conclusion

The political polarization of education has made the jobs of education leaders and teachers nearly impossible. Think tanks have weaponized emotions and fear, prompting people to speak out against inclusive and equitable education materials in school board meetings, whether their children attend that district or not.[41] This places superintendents in complicated positions, as one superintendent explains: "We've had to be far more nimble and creative than I think we ever had to be before, and we've had to do it under even more intense pressure and criticism in a job that was already subject to a lot of pressure and criticism."[42]

Dismantling manufactured fear and false narratives with evidence-based messaging allows leaders to build relationships with communities and families, increase transparency, and give voice to the equitable education approaches most families support.

CHAPTER 6

Psychological Implications of the Anti-Critical Race Theory Movement on Black Children

Jessica T. DeCuir-Gunby

In 2020, Donald Trump issued an executive order to "combat offensive and Anti-American race and sex stereotyping and scapegoating" by federal contractors and in federal agencies.[1] Since then, at least forty-four states have introduced anti-critical race theory (CRT) or diversity legislation that limits how teachers can talk about race in schools, with eighteen states having imposed some type of legislation.[2] The state of Florida has been a leader in the anti-CRT movement, having passed the infamous House Bill 7 (HB7) to protect white children against "woke indoctrination" in schools. In reaction to the passing of the bill, Florida Governor Ron DeSantis stated in a news release, "No one should be instructed to feel as if they are not equal or shamed because of their race."[3]

As a part of this movement, Florida has even banned the teaching of AP African American Studies because of its supposed connections to CRT, asserting that the course lacks "educational value and historical accuracy."[4] Further, Florida has changed the state's African American history standards by minimizing the impact of racism and sanitizing the experiences of African Americans. For example, the standards suggest that violence during Reconstruction was "perpetrated against and by African Americans."[5]

Florida legislators, as well as many legislators across the country, seem to only be concerned about the perspectives and experiences of white students in schools. However, it is important to recognize that the implications of these laws extend beyond white children. What about students of color, particularly Black children? These anti-CRT laws, which seem to disproportionately target Black children, convey a distressing message that their experiences do not matter; that their feelings do not matter; that they do not matter. What impact will these policy changes have on Black children? This chapter centers the experiences of Black children, considering the potentially negative psychological consequences of efforts to ban racial truth-telling in schools. I also recommend strategies that families and educators can employ to mitigate the impact of these efforts.

How the Anti-CRT Movement Psychologically Harms Black Children

The impact of racism on the psychological development of African Americans has been well documented.[6] Some of the earliest work, including the now-classic baby doll research studies conducted by Kenneth and Mamie Clark in the 1930s–1950s, demonstrated how racial segregation and racism promoted a negative self-concept, having a deleterious effect on the racial identity development of Black children. The findings of this research were so profound that it was cited in footnote 11 of the *Brown v. Board of Education* decision as supporting evidence to end racial segregation in schools.[7] Now, seventy years past the *Brown* decision, Black children still face threats to their sense of Black identity and psychological safety. The anti-CRT initiatives and anti-Black messages accompanying them have the potential to cause Black children tremendous psychological harm, such as racial, physiological/neurological, and generational trauma.

Racial Trauma

Black children are continuously bombarded by negative racial messages, images, and stereotypes in society. For example, it is common to hear stories, read commentaries, or see images of Black people being portrayed as aggressive, hyper-sexual, anti-intellectual, or unattractive. It is even common to see Black people being victimized by state-sanctioned authorities, including the police, such as in the case of George Floyd. These stereotypes exist and are perpetuated, often within the school context, because of systemic racism and white supremacy. Yet the anti-CRT initiatives being implemented within schools are banning the very discussion of how these stereotypes evolved and are maintained. The anti-CRT initiatives further amplify these negative racial messages and stereotypes within the school context, causing Black children to endure race-based stress or racial trauma—constant experiencing of racial harm or discrimination, whether actual, perceived, or vicarious.[8] Racial trauma is experienced differently during developmental periods and is influenced by the intensity or the magnitude of the event(s).[9] For example, a preschool-aged child (three to five years old) may not have the cognitive capability to verbalize their experience with racial trauma and may instead react by exhibiting developmentally regressive behavior such as bed wetting. On the other hand, a high school-aged child (fourteen to seventeen) that experiences racial trauma generally understands the concept of racism and what they are experiencing and may engage in help-seeking behaviors or delinquent behaviors. Regardless, experiencing racial trauma in childhood and adolescence, as well as the severity of the racial trauma, can have a lasting impact, influencing adult health outcomes. Research has found strong associations between racial discrimination and mental health outcomes as well as behavioral issues such as aggression, risk-taking, and self-harming behavior such as substance abuse.[10]

Physiological/Neurological Trauma

In addition to causing racial trauma, the anti-CRT initiatives can contribute to Black children experiencing physiological trauma, including neurological trauma. Sustained exposure to racial stress or trauma can have a major impact on the body. Research has demonstrated that prolonged exposure to racial trauma is associated with poor cardiovascular health outcomes such as high blood pressure, vascular risk factors, heart attack, and stroke.[11] Racial trauma has also been linked to poor birth outcomes, including increased preterm birth, low birth weight, and high maternal morbidity and mortality.[12] In addition to physical challenges, including racial stress, long-term experiences of trauma can have a negative neurological impact on children. Prolonged stress such as racial trauma can cause functional changes and remodeling of the brain architecture, potentially impacting behavioral development, neurological development, and/or memory.[13] As demonstrated, implementing the anti-CRT initiatives has the potential to be detrimental to the long-term mental and physical well-being of Black children.

Generational Trauma

Reading any Black history book, it is easy to see how every generation of Black people in the United States has endured collective racial trauma.[14] The anti-CRT movement is yet another manifestation of this collective racial trauma. Past racial trauma can significantly impact individuals in a variety of ways. New research on transgenerational epigenetic inheritance illustrates how ancestral exposure to trauma can impact descendants across generations, including the manifestation of health disparities.[15] The impact of racism can be manifested physiologically, impacting body chemistry, hormones, cells, and fibers, then passed along across generations. In other words, persistent health disparities (e.g., low birth weight) can be partially explained by the racial trauma experienced by a person's ancestors.

Understanding the impact of systemic racism and racial discrimination—spanning from slavery to Reconstruction, Jim Crow, the Civil Rights Movement, and to the present—reveals that Black children have already inherited considerable racial trauma from previous generations. Any racial trauma stemming from their experiences with the anti-CRT movement has the potential to be compounded, thus perpetuating a vicious cycle. Black children are poised to experience racial trauma from the anti-CRT movement (and in their daily lives), adding to the racial trauma that they have already inherited, and being prepped to pass their racial trauma to the next generation. As an example, a Black public high school student in Florida can no longer take her school's AP African American History and AP Psychology courses because they were banned by the state's anti-CRT legislation. This could cause her racial trauma. In addition, she witnessed various acts of anti-Black violence during the Black Lives Matter protests and suffers from chronic asthma because she lives in a low socio economic status (SES) area near a county incinerator. Direct experiences with racism, such as environmental racism, could cause her additional racial trauma. Transgenerational epigenetic inheritance suggests that some of the racial trauma that she is experiencing might be inherited from her ancestors and that the racial trauma she is currently experiencing will most likely be transmitted to her descendants.

How to Counter the Psychological Harm
Caused by the Anti-CRT Movement
Through Racial Truth-Telling

Although these anti-CRT policies have the potential to inflict substantial psychological harm on Black children, there are many ways that parents, teachers, counselors, and community members can become involved to help mitigate the negative impact. By collectively working together to address these concerns through racial truth-telling, the influence of these damaging initiatives can be lessened. In this section, I outline strategies to promote racial pride, reduce racial stress, and challenge anti-CRT initiatives to safeguard the mental well-being of Black children.

Promoting Racial Pride

One of the most important ways to challenge the negative impact of the anti-CRT initiatives is to help Black children to develop a strong sense of Black racial identity. Black children need to understand who they are as Black people and to feel good about being Black. They need to develop a strong sense of racial pride. One way to help develop racial pride is through racial socialization or "how African American parents maintain children's high self-esteem and prepare them to understand racial barriers given systems of racial stratification in the United States."[16]

Parents must engage in racial truth-telling. They should actively educate their children about who they are as Black people, the historical collective struggle of Black people, and the pervasive impact of systemic racism and white supremacy. Also, teaching Black children about their own family history is important to developing a connection to the Black community.[17] Providing culturally affirming experiences such as reading books by and about Black people, going to Black cultural museums, and attending Black plays and concerts, can further solidify a sense of racial pride.

Reducing Racial Stress

Another essential way to challenge the negative impact of the anti-CRT initiatives is to help Black children reduce race-related stress. The debates surrounding the anti-CRT initiatives have been anything but peaceful. At meetings where these initiatives have been discussed, there has been name calling, shouting matches, and even physical altercations. Experiencing or hearing about the vitriol associated with the anti-CRT initiatives and debates can be very stressful for Black children. Also, learning about the racism experienced by Black people can be emotionally difficult for some Black children. Because of this, it is imperative that parents and counselors help Black children develop better coping skills, particularly racial coping skills or "learning to positively reappraise a DRE [discriminatory racial encounter] as less threatening and make decisions during racial encounters that are choices, not reactions."[18]

These skills include armoring, which involves developing pride in personal talents and abilities, collective coping/activism and finding support from others with like-minded individuals and organizations, sponsorship and mentorship to empower through mentoring relationships, and engaging in self-care by eating healthy foods and engaging in physical activity.[19]

Another way to help Black children reduce race-related stress is to encourage them to limit their social media exposure. There is a lot of information and discourse about the anti-CRT movement online, where exposure to racial discrimination can negatively impact the mental health of Black children.[20] Limiting the amount of time that Black children spend online will greatly reduce the amount of racism-related stress they experience.

Challenging Anti-CRT Initiatives

It is also important for community members to become involved in supporting Black children. Educational institutions, particularly K–12 schools, can play an important role. While they have been the focus of much of the anti-CRT movement, educators work to mitigate negative effects on Black children. First, educators need to study the anti-CRT laws that have been passed in their states/counties, learn what the laws explicitly state, and then map out plans for what can and cannot be done in schools.

Educators only need to follow the law; they should not be adding to the law. It is imperative that they do not completely abandon teaching diversity issues. There is a lot that teachers can still teach while also following any imposed legislation. For example, each state requires that teachers teach according to their respective state's standards. State teaching standards outlines what needs to be taught but not how the information should be taught, leaving room for incorporating issues of diversity and equity. Even in the case of Florida's African American history standards, there are a lot of areas where educators can teach about the real experiences and contributions of African Americans. For instance, one standard states to "understand the causes, course, and consequences of the Civil War and Reconstruction and its effects on the American people."[21] Teachers can focus on the racism experienced by and perpetrated against Black people during those time periods. To do so, teachers must be committed to teaching students the real and factual history. They must be committed to engaging in racial truth-telling.

There are additional ways to support racial truth-telling in schools. Parents can support teachers by supplementing the school curriculum with culturally relevant materials within the home and should ask teachers for suggested resource materials. Educators can also advocate for diversity initiatives that are not directly banned in legislation. For instance, secondary English teachers can promote books by Black authors, being careful not to select books that are on the banned book list. In addition, not every state or county is in support of the anti-CRT initiatives. Those entities that support diversity should be courageous enough to pass prodiversity bills in education. For instance, in 2021, California passed Assembly Bill 101, making ethnic studies a requirement for high school graduation. Principalities across the country should create legislation to counter all the antidiversity initiatives. This would show Black children and children of color in general that there are communities that value who they are as well as their experiences.

Conclusion

With the rise of the Black Lives Matter movement in response to the police killings of innocent Black people, many organizations, businesses, and individuals felt compelled to take a stand, even engaging in self-reflection and creating calls to act against structural racism. For example, racism was declared a threat to public health by the American Medical Association, the American Academy of Pediatrics, and other health-care organizations.[22] The American Psychological Association went as far as apologizing for their ignoring and promotion of systemic racism.[23] Now that the anti-CRT movement is pushing forward, many of these same organizations, businesses, and individuals have been silent. It's time for everyone to recommit. The anti-CRT initiatives are leading to another serious public health crisis. We cannot be afraid to challenge the anti-CRT movement, because too much is at stake. We must make the psychological health and safety of Black children a priority.

CHAPTER 7

Realities for Queer Students of Color in the Age of Suppressing Racial Truth-Telling

Antonio Duran

The present moment in the United States has seen a growth of targeted attacks against racial truth-telling in K–12 schools and higher education institutions, furthering the marginalization of people of color as a result. Happening concurrently with these efforts are also movements to strip queer and trans individuals of their rights, including within educational settings. One does not need to look far to find legislation such as the "Don't Say Gay Bill" that is happening in state contexts like Florida, which scholars have argued will have devastating effects on queer and trans educators and students[1]. Yet it is important that educators not view these issues as distinctive, for both of these are designed to uphold the white supremacist, heterosexist, and transphobic foundations of US educational settings. And significantly, the targeting of content that exposes these multiple truths (i.e., related to race, sexuality, and gender) only serves to disenfranchise students with multiple minoritized identities—specifically, queer and trans students of color (QTSOC).

In this chapter, I describe how individuals should not see this moment of suppressing racial truth-telling as disconnected from attacks of queer-antagonism and trans-antagonism but, rather, as drastically intertwined tactics to subjugate multiply minoritized groups. To elaborate on this argument, I first begin by drawing threads together between the emphasis on suppressing racial truth telling in the United States and legislative movements to strip queer and trans people from their rights. I then articulate the consequences that this particular period has on QTSOC across K–12 and higher education contexts. I finally conclude by offering specific recommendations for educators and those hoping to support queer and trans students, especially those with multiple minoritized identities.

Interconnectedness of Racial Truth Suppression and Queer/Trans-Antagonism

To begin, I find it necessary to describe how the work that is happening to suppress racial truth-telling is not separate from what queer and trans individuals are experiencing in the United States and beyond. This argument is at the core of the work of intersectional theorists who have showcased the need to consider how the law and policy often reinforce single-axis discrimination thinking, in which systems of racism and sexism are thought of in discrete ways[2]. And yet, this type of framing is reductive and fails to capture the experiences of those who feel the effects of overlapping and coconstituting systems of oppression. What this signifies is that resistance against the racialized suppression that those in the United States are witnessing must require attention to how this affects those with multiple minoritized identities, potentially using frames like that proposed by Dean Spade when he argued for intersectional reform.[3]

Of note, scholars both in and out of higher education have showcased how people have used white supremacy to describe who is perceived as normative, which has implications for surveilling gender and sexuality. In other words, with whiteness comes standards for how people perform their other identities appropriately, which has served to oppress queer and trans people throughout history. For instance, critical legal theorists like Darren Hutchinson[4] have demonstrated that antiracist policy discussions have often minimized the marginalization of queer and trans communities and, at worst, perpetuated this oppression. This occurs by maintaining values of heteronormativity, patriarchy, and gendered roles.

Within higher education, D.-L. Stewart and Z. Nicolazzo have demonstrated how whiteness serves as a container that further pushes trans students to the margins, and more specifically, trans students of color—especially in conversations about high-impact practices.[5] In presenting high-impact practices that are applied to all students, whiteness enforces boundaries on who is considered a successful student, alienating trans students and QTSOC. The same also proves to be true in the inverse. In fact, scholars such as Marquéz and Brockenbrough have demonstrated how lawsuits entailing antiqueer bias within K–12 settings have failed to consider any racialized dynamics involved in the cases.[6]

What is emphasized through these examples is that people often do not view the suppression of racial truth-telling as contributing to the oppression of queer and trans people; and yet, it does so in explicit and implicit ways. Similarly, queer- and trans-antagonism does not exist separately, but rather, frequently furthers the marginalization of communities of color. In the section that follows, I unpack how the disinformation that is being spread as a result of legislative efforts will have harmful effects on QTSOC both in K–12 and in higher education settings.

Consequences for Queer and Trans Students of Color

Given their positioning at the intersections of multiple systems of oppression, QTSOC are particularly affected by contemporary legislative battles. The marginalization that these students face only exemplifies the erasure of QTSOC that frequently occurs both in higher education[7] and in K–12 settings.[8] What is consistent in the literature about QTSOC is that they experience an amplified sense of marginalization as they face not just the effects of racism, heterosexism, and trans oppression, but importantly, the impacts of these systems overlapping and coconstituting one another. Examples of this may include feeling a lack of belongingness in educational settings not simply because of how whiteness may permeate campus, but also because of how heterosexism and trans oppression are upheld through interactions, policies, and practices.

In the suppression of racial truth-telling, students of color are being denied the opportunity to learn about how the inequities they report are systemic as opposed to simply an individual problem. Moreover, conversations about how racism encodes structures like heterosexism, gendered expectations, and trans oppression are nowhere to be found. When disinformation is spread about race, so too are race's complex connections to other identities eradicated. Hence, QTSOC may believe that a harmful interaction that occurs in school is a problem that they caused as opposed to contextualizing such interpersonal actions within broader systems that are targeting them. Suppressing racial truths also minimizes the plight of QTSOC who have been pushed to the margins, including within communities of color themselves, because of deference to whiteness. It is common for QTSOC to face marginalization not simply within educational settings more generally, but also specifically within race- or ethnicity-based spaces or LGBTQ+ groups. Refusals to accept QTSOC may emerge from the fear of already being seen as deviant due to their race/ethnicity and the fear that further perceptions of abnormality tied to queerness will exacerbate marginalization.

Consequences also exist in formalized spaces and curriculum within educational contexts. Even in states that allow for inclusive K–12 curricula, educators may still reify whiteness by failing to consider the needs of QTSOC, and specifically, Black LGBTQ+ youth.[9] Thus, considering legislative moves that suppress racial truths, one can assume that even if a state allows LGBTQ+ curricula, QTSOC will not see their experiences represented in educational settings. The same is true for LGBTQ+ services on college campuses (e.g., LGBTQ+ centers), as scholars have written about the whiteness that often permeates such spaces.[10] Educators can consequently not rely on the belief that QTSOC will still find support for their identities, as discussions on racism are being evaded and erased by legislators.

Although the present attacks can have devastating effects on the lives of QTSOC, it is imperative to not see these students in a deficit light, portraying them as powerless in the face of governmental actions. Rather, QTSOC have historically found ways to assert their agency,[11] and they will continue to do so in spite of these challenges. Scholars like Dozono have named how QTOSC establish worlds for themselves through their literacy practices in the classroom and have shown that, in the absence of being able to access this in curricular spaces, it is likely that they will move elsewhere. QTSOC have continuously practiced agency. With this knowledge in mind, it is my assertion that educators can be key institutional agents that enable these students' resilience and agency, working alongside them in spite of contemporary challenges.

Recommendations and Considerations for Educators

Considering that the moves toward suppressing racial truthtelling have impacts on QTSOC, in addition to the legislative attacks on queer and trans rights, the question of what one can do to support queer and trans students of color emerges. Although any recommendations are inherently dependent on other factors (e.g., geographical region and institutional context) and incomplete, it is my desire to offer a few suggestions that can equip educators with ideas and strategies that they can implement to uplift QTSOC within their schools, colleges, and universities and local settings.

Because it is not fair to assume that educators are aware of what QTSOC report as their experiences in educational settings, a significant first step needs to entail finding access to information that details how QTSOC navigate schools, colleges, and universities. For instance, GLSEN has a series of resource guides that describe how distinct racial/ethnic groups who identify as queer and trans report their experiences in educational settings, recognizing that differences are present even within the QTSOC umbrella.[12] Hence, educators should engage in personal development and learning about what QTSOC require.

Related to gaining awareness about what QTOSC individuals need, it is vital that educators then consider what roles they are willing to play in advocating for QTSOC within their local settings. One would be remiss to not contextualize a conversation about advocating for these students devoid of the risks and consequences that come with it (e.g., being fired or losing out on career mobility). Consequently, educators must be cognizant of what they are willing to lose. They also should consider whether it is appropriate to provide students with readings that may be helpful in actualizing their identity exploration, even if those texts are banned. Creating informal spaces for these students to connect with each other may be useful for their belongingness and persistence. Literature on being tempered radicals and on coalition-building can offer useful frameworks and guidance, as it highlights how resistance and advocacy can take many forms.[13]

When educators in K–12 schools, colleges, and universities encounter legislative acts that constrain their ability to teach about communities of color, as well as about queer and trans groups, it can be difficult to imagine the possibility of engaging in direct actions within these settings. While this is indeed the case in far too many locales, educators can partner with local community organizations to attend to the needs of QTSOC. Researchers such as Marquéz[14] have offered ways to do this. In addition, community groups could offer QTSOC educational, communal, and liberatory spaces that are not available on their campuses. Attached to this recommendation is exploring the power of virtual communities that QTSOC can turn to in these moments.

Finally, in a time when people of color, as well as queer and trans individuals, are experiencing continued marginalization, it is crucial to not let this define their realities. As noted above, QTSOC have long practiced acts of agency and resilience in the face of oppression. What is often missing from discussions of centering the needs of queer and trans people of color is uplifting their joy.[15] Thus, it is vital that educators find opportunities to allow QTSOC to express queer joy, vitality, and well-being. Whether these spaces are within school and college environments, in local communities off campus, or in virtual and digital spaces, they may differ based on the educator's comfort or the context in which individuals are located. However, it is my wish that readers take steps, whether subversive or explicit, to design initiatives that amplify the joy that QTSOC embody.

Conclusion

As QTSOC progressively encounter amplified marginalization in different states and locales, educators hold the key to advocating for these individuals. The suppression of racial truth-telling inevitably intersects with other systems of oppression that affect queer and trans students of color, meaning that individuals must pay attention to these over-lapping structures of inequity. When advocating against the suppression of racial truth-telling, it is crucial to attend to the disenfranchisement of QTSOC and those who are often left out of the conversation.

CHAPTER 8

Visions of Black Liberation for Teachers in an Era of Distorted Truths

Justin A. Coles

In this chapter, I examine visions of Black liberation for teaching and teacher education for students being educated in what the poet Elizabeth Alexander refers to as the "Trayvon generation." Grounded in the Black Liberation in Teacher Education (BLiTE) framework,[1] I explore Black liberation as a way to unearth the true realities of education in an anti-Black nation while providing concrete actions and recommendations for educators to commit to building liberatory schools and classrooms to disrupt Black death and destruction.

Legacies of Black Terror and the Distortion of Truths

I still think of Trayvon Martin's body lying cold and dead in the rain. As a millennial Black man who is a descendant of those enslaved on the white settler colonial lands of the United States, I am no stranger to images of Black death. Four years before I was born, Philadelphia Police launched a targeted attack against The Movement (MOVE) organization on May 13, 1985, which resulted in shooting ten thousand rounds of ammunition from automatic weapons, machine guns, and antitank guns and dropping a bomb on the members' residence (a row house), which resulted in the death of five adult MOVE members and six children. The MOVE bombing, which resulted in 61 homes being destroyed and 250 people being left unhoused, took place less than 3 miles from the house in which I was raised. Being in such proximity to MOVE, including the ways I was educated about the bombing as I grew into Black boyhood, has given the images of Osage Avenue burning to the ground residence in my mind. I have looked at the images and video footage so much throughout my lifetime that I often feel my body has a sort of ancestral memory of that time and place, almost giving me the ability to smell the fiery smoke and the burning of a Black neighborhood as a way to remember that I am immersed in a climate of anti-Blackness.

Two years after my birth, Rodney King was severely beaten by Los Angeles police, captured on video camera footage by a bystander who lived in the neighborhood where he was pulled over. The images of Rodney's face are also permanently imprinted in my mind, a part of my individual and collective Black ancestral/historical knowledge. I often feel as if I can hear the clubs and batons striking his flesh and that I can see the ghoulish faces of the officers, who were all acquitted of any criminal charges, beating him ruthlessly. So, you see, I am no stranger to the abundance of violence that greets Black people on lands where they were once enslaved as chattel and commodities—and where they are still living in the wake of such terror and destruction.[2] Yet the death of Trayvon strikes me out of all of the stories of Black violence under conditions of white settler terror, because it was not a story I was told, but rather a story that I witnessed unfold.

Searching for Understanding: Anti-Blackness and Miseducation in Educator Preparation

I received my doctoral degree in curriculum, instruction, and teacher education from a program that has consistently ranked number one in the nation for educator preparation. I attended my program because I wanted to engage deeply in understanding the relationship Blackness has with curriculum, and more specifically, the ways teachers were trained (or not trained) to be attentive to matters of race and racial oppression. I quickly realized that at the highest level of preparing doctoral students to train teachers there was a severe lack of knowledge dissemination that explicitly oriented us to understanding teaching and learning as highly politicized in a societal context where anti-Blackness is endemic, shaping the schooling experiences of Black and non-Black students and educators in harmful ways. While there were courses and research and teaching experiences that we could engage in that did make us aware of such social contexts, the core foundation of my doctoral studies was not grounded in this awareness—and we were definitely not trained to prepare teachers to engage in actions to disrupt anti-Blackness in curriculum.

Given that I began my degree in August 2013 as the trial for the murderer of Trayvon was unfolding, I was searching to develop my understanding of the ways the field of teacher education was attentive to the structural regime of anti-Blackness and the ways it informs curriculum development and larger educative processes and interactions (e.g., teacher dispositions, student behavior systems, access to updated resources, etc.). My goal here is not to indict my doctoral program specifically. Rather, my aim in this chapter is to critique the way educator preparation at-large can and must do a better job at protecting the livelihoods of Black youth given the ways Blackness is historically and structurally marginalized in classrooms. I believe that turning to visions of Black liberation philosophies can serve as a corrective pathway toward dispelling distorted truths and committing to actionable methods to create schools that acknowledge anti-Blackness at the very least and fiercely disrupting it at best.

Trayvon Martin and a (Re)commitment to Truth-Telling

Trayvon Martin's death, just like the deaths of MOVE members and the beating of Rodney King, was distorted by anti-Black truths. Narratives about Trayvon's literal Black existence were communicated through lenses of criminality, dehumanization, and unfounded fear logics that can be directly traced to histories and ideologies that have long sought and still seek to socially construct Black being as inherently dangerous and therefore deserving of un/imaginable violence. While Black people and communities have experienced anti-Black violence long before and well after the MOVE bombing and Rodney King beating, the murder of Trayvon inaugurated a contemporary era where white vigilante and police officer violence resurged as an everyday topic in US life. In Black communities, this came less in the form of a resurgence in conversation and more in the form of a deepening (re)commitment to truth-telling about the realities of anti-Black terror. Black people had to organize themselves to resist neoliberal, post-racial dialogue that pushed diversity and multiculturalism discourse to the fore of the US body politic as a way to say that race no longer structures society and its institutions.

While overt white supremacist and anti-Black discourse may have been removed from public policy documents, it was replaced with an unwritten doctrine of white educational and cultural supremacy," which makes organizing for Black liberation in our current societal moment more crucial.[3] This (re)commitment to truth-telling became particularly evident in the moment of Trayvon's murder since the nation was under the leadership of the country's first Black president, which for many signaled a falsehood that Black people were unrestricted by their race and anti-Black racism. I am not communicating that Black people were not dying at the hands of police and vigilante citizens prior to Trayvon (as they were and continue to do so). Rather, I am articulating how the death of Trayvon ushered in a new phase of hyper-visible deaths of unarmed Black people (back) into the psyche of the US citizenry, in ways that forced the country to directly engage in examinations of anti-Blackness.

Black Liberation and the Politics of Truth-Telling: A Black Education Imperative

Beyond the vigilante murder of Trayvon by a white Hispanic male serving as a reminder to the US public about the disposability of Black life, in a society where anti-Blackness is endemic, it also reminded me of how Black disposability is mirrored in our nation's schools.[4] More importantly, Trayvon's death, which occurred during my time as an eighth-grade literature teacher to predominately Black and Brown children, led me to turn to the necessity of centering Black liberation in the move toward equity and justice in our teaching and learning processes as a political method for disrupting anti-Blackness. A major standpoint in Black education is "the realization and acknowledgement for a large number of Blacks that all education is unequivocally political and Black education can ill afford to be less so."[5] Thus, for those invested in countering distorted truths informed by anti-Black ideologies and practices, understanding truth-telling as political is a necessity. As Darnell Ragland notes, "truth-telling can reveal historical exclusions," and we "need to more actively engage truth-telling particularly vis-à-vis Black experiences and liberation struggles."[6] How does engaging in Black liberation in teaching and learning rupture the distorted truths about Black people and communities in schools? How do we cultivate teacher education to become a site of formal truth-telling processes?

When the news of Trayvon's murder picked up mainstream media coverage, I remember walking into my school building that week and feeling the air heavy with grief, shock, and confusion. For the majority of my Black students, this would be their first hyper-visible, highly politicized (and polarizing) unarmed Black death that they were alive to experience. Also, since I was teaching at a school that served grades 7–12, the students were close in age to Trayvon or his exact age. It is also important to note, as mentioned previously, that the students were living in a time where there was a Black president and much of the US political discourse focused on decentering race and racism from national conversations, despite their enduring existence as structural barriers to living. The confusion that I sensed the students in my school were feeling became even more present as days and weeks went by and they became aware that the media was taking more interest in finding ways to discredit and criminalize Trayvon than in investigating the murderer's background or motives. For instance, on the 911 call from the man who murdered Trayvon, which was released to the public, it was clear that he was using racially coded language to describe Trayvon.[7] The concept that a Black teen walking home in the rain while on the phone was "suspicious," "up to no good," and "on drugs" is fueled by anti-Black anecdotes, which image Blackness and Black people as bad and perpetual threats to the nation-state.

Even in matters of diversity and inclusion in educational spaces, Blackness can be seen as disruptive or as not willing to fit neatly into ideals of a collective people of color progress. Any of my students could have been anywhere in the US walking in the rain with a hoodie, skittles, and snacks and have been stalked, chased, and then shot dead, under the assumption that they were a danger to society, as with Trayvon. I immediately began to think about the ways US teaching and learning processes, and particularly US schooling as a site of punishment and a containment apparatus for Black children, also function to uphold and facilitate harm against Black youth.[8] As Jones reminds us, the story of struggling against destructive educative processes "begins with the first Africans to set foot in the New World."[9] In fact, slaves demanded their education well before emancipation and were responsible for creating "a system of public education available to *all* children."[10]

Black Humanity, Possibility, and Desire in the Era of Black Lives Matter

In thinking about the destruction schools have caused Black youth and communities since the foundation of modern public schooling as we know it, I then began to think less about damage and more about the legacies of possibility and desire (to create and cultivate liberatory existences) Black people have created through engaging in Black liberatory educational politics.[11] As David Chevannes and Juan Lopez note, to become liberatory, Blackness "must ground itself in an educative praxis that has both decolonial and anti-imperial inflections. To do so, in concrete terms, means valorizing, or more aptly, the mattering of Black lives."[12] Historically, Black scholars have communicated that for Black education to be meaningful in an anti-Black society, educators must assist Black (and non-Black) students "in developing an awareness of the forces of racism and colonialism with its psychological, sociological, and physical oppression.[13] Darnell Ragland undergirds the importance of Black liberation efforts being decolonial and anti-imperial, noting that "colonial structures deny the personhood of non-White people and truth-telling challenges that narrative."[14]

The truth of existing in a slave nation (present tense, as slavery was/is a structure that lingers and still organizes everyday social realities) is that Black life is considered disposable; not by happenstance, but the disposability of Black life has been concretized through a networking of ideologies, laws, polices, pseudo-science, and social interactions. To dream up new visions of Black liberation (informed by the past, present, and future projected realities/desires of Black life), "truth-telling is especially important given the failure of legal systems to uphold laws meant to protect Black communities."[15] Due to "the ongoing silence around the history of U.S. slavery and colonization" disrupting distorted truths "matters deeply because of the permanent enshrinement of spaces for subtle and outright discrimination" that organize the nation's institutions and social interactions.[16]

Distorted truths—truths that seek to uphold and benefit dominant power structures and to oppress Black people while maintaining the status quo—deny the nation's anti-Black roots by suppressing Black voices and lived experience, which makes it easier to blame Black people and communities for their marginalized status. Black Lives Matter is an ideological and political intervention in a world where Black lives are systematically and intentionally targeted for demise. It is an affirmation of Black folks' humanity, our contributions to this society, and our resilience in the face of deadly oppression. The current movement for Black lives is grounded in truth-telling through relying on foundations of Black liberation, which upholds "the necessity to reclaim [Black] history and [Black] identity from the cultural terrorism and depredation of self-justifying white guilt."[17] Moreover, the Black liberation qualities of Black Lives Matter become evident when we understand the movement as "an attempt at social and political reeducation by interrogating and, ultimately, disclaiming the Euro-American valuelessness affixed to Black lives."[18]

Visioning Black liberation in teacher education is wholly a matter of reeducation. Historicizing anti-Blackness and developing strategic actions to counter the ways it informs our entire social system, particularly schools and curriculum, is essential. As an educator concerned with the preparation of our nation's teachers, understanding Black liberation to disrupt distorted truths that negatively impact students' experiences in school and society is a matter of life or death for me. Using the phrase "life or death" is not meant to serve as an exaggeration, but to capture the very real ways the proliferation of misinformation about a community can result in tangible violence against Black psyches and bodies.

A major underlying logic for distorted anti-Black truths is the ideal that Black people are nonhuman/superhuman—either a thing (e.g., a commodity to be owned) or a being with capacities beyond knowable human strength (e.g., tolerating inhumane levels of pain).[19] Black liberation traditions work against such fallacies to recognize and defend "the unique contribution that people of African ancestry have to make to civilization and humanity."[20] Given the link between education and freedom, teachers must familiarize themselves with the ways anti-Blackness prompts conditions of unfreedom for Black students and engage in methods that work toward freedom.[21] Foundational to freedom efforts must be focusing on *Black humanity* under conditions of white violence and highlighting "how the promise of freedom guaranteed under U.S. law of life, liberty, and the pursuit of happiness often eludes Black people."[22]

Black Liberation in Teacher Education: A Framework to Dispel Distorted Truths

If anti-Blackness positions Black people to live in a social context where their humanity, particularly the goodness or value of their humanity, is continually in question or dismissed, I would say that Black liberation works to dispel the false truths of Blackness having no value. Black liberation is wholly about rejecting external, dominant gazes of whiteness that seek to define what Blackness is and is not. The act of liberating comes into being through the ways Black people come to name and define who they are for their own selves. This is not to say that efforts of Black liberation cancel out anti-Blackness and anti-Black gazes that seek to position Black people as inherently marginal and inferior, but those liberatory efforts do birth a politics that sharpens the consciousness of Black people, and here Black educators, to refuse violent truths that can only exist through the destruction of Black minds and bodies.

How might truth-telling in the Black liberation tradition author new and future visions of educational justice? Gathered from a survey of literature on Black teacher practices, liberation, and Back education, my colleague Darrius Stanley and I strive to begin answering this question through what we conceptualize as a framework for Black Liberation in Teacher Education (BLiTE).[23] In the next section, I detail the five pillars of BLiTE in relation to dispelling distorted truths informed by anti-Blackness, particularly highlighting how the framework can be put into practice.

The Five Pillars of BLiTE

To help teachers and teacher educators move toward truth-telling practices as they relate to countering anti-Blackness, I share the five pillars of the BLiTE framework: (1) resistance and subversion, (2) spiritual innovation, (3) intersectionality, (4) Black fugitive thought, and (5) Afrofuturism. The organizing principles that undergird BLiTE are joy and restoration, particularly thinking about the ways anti-Blackness quite literally seeks to suppress both concepts. In our initial conception of BLiTE, we explained, "At the center of Black liberatory thought, which has been used as a compass to cultural sustainability, lies Black joy and/as restoration. Black liberation is grounded in the belief that being Black is not terrible (but a gift), which catalyzes the creation of methods and actions to re/claim power over one's life and education in ways that bring about a culturally restorative joy."[24] The pillars of BLiTE are not exhaustive, but they do serve as over-arching frames that work to structure the ways Black liberation thought and praxis are present throughout the history of Black education. In figure 8.1, I detail the five pillars with descriptions of each pillar and tangible ways these can be used to prepare educators to engage Black liberation to disrupt distorted truths that work to oppress the academic lives of Black students.

Resistance and subversion capture the ways Black people leverage informal and formal educational opportunities as a pathway to self/determination in spite of the ways the US schooling landscape has been grounded in anti-Blackness. In the face of oppressive policies such as antiliteracy laws, school segregation, and exclusionary and punitive discipline measures, Black communities committed to education as a site of freedom away from physical and psychological bondage. Thinking with resistance and subversion to counter anti-Black truths, educators should make sure their practices include "Black counterstories that detail the histories of Black social movements around education that have worked to lay the foundation for access to education for all within

BLACK LIBERATION IN TEACHER EDUCATION

DESCRIPTIONS OF PILLARS AND RECOMMENDATIONS FOR TEACHERS

RESISTANCE AND SUBVERSION

Description:
Leveraging pedagogies as forms of resistance to and subversion of anti-Black policies, procedures, and curricula.

Read: From *BlackLivesMatter to Black Liberation* by Keeanga-Yamahtta Taylor

SPIRITUAL INNOVATION

Description:
Understanding how Black spirituality informs hope, freedom-dreaming, and consciousness-raising educational praxis.

Read: *The Cross and the Lynching Tree* by James H. Cone

INTERSECTIONALITY

Description:
Engaging students' multiple, under theorized margins of identity by challenging white supremacist, hetero-patriarchal, binary, homo/trans-phobias.

Read: *Demarginalizing the Intersection of Race and Sex* by Kimberlé Crenshaw

BLACK FUGITIVE THOUGHT

Description:
Cultivating and/or supporting classroom spaces that refuse Black confinement through building future-forward actions that dislodge students from anti-Black schooling processes.

Read: *Listening to Images* by Tina M. Campt

AFROFUTURISM

Description:
Centering a Black-specific visioning that spans the past, present, and future that declares that Black life has and will always matter to the nation's future development.

Read: *Afrofuturism 2.0: The Rise of Astro-Blackness* by Reynaldo Anderson and Charles E. Jones

Figure 8.1 BLiTE framework descriptions and recommendations

this country."[25] A major component of distorted truths is the absence of stories from communities on the receiving end of violence, which allows for mainstream narratives to flourish unchallenged. Resistance and subversion must start with being informed by practices that call into question anti-Black violence that has been normalized over time.

Spiritual innovation represents the inextricable link between the Black church as a political and educational institution, which catalyzed and sustained Black liberation efforts. Black spirituality—a spiritual consciousness—prompts a unique standpoint of faith and consciousness-raising in an anti-Black society as a core component in movements launched to counter anti-Blackness. Black spirituality directly helped Black people navigate the harshness of the nation's schooling environments while providing Black educators and community leaders with the self-awareness to engage in pedagogies that uplifted Black students. Teachers and teacher educators committed to dispelling false truths that cause harm to Black students "must engage the pedagogies and philosophies that are intertwined with Black spirituality" by "possessing an awareness of how Black spiritual innovation has served as a central liberatory tool in the Black educational struggle."[26] Educators do not need to become experts or practitioners of Black spiritual practices, but if they take the concrete step to learn about community and uplift it as sacred and essential to Black truth-telling, they can lead to the development of practices that counter individualist ideals meant to separate rather than unite.

Originally conceptualized to name the specific experience of being both Black and a woman, intersectionality is a key pillar in education liberation efforts to understand the various ways Black students may experience anti-Black oppression differently based on their varying identity markers (e.g., gender, sexuality, ethnicity, skin color, dis/ability, etc.). All too often, conceptions of Black cultural responsiveness in schools can be enacted in ways that deny how Blackness is lived across multiple intersections, further marginalizing students and causing harm. To engage intersectionality in concrete terms is not simply about acknowledging the multiple identities of Black being. Rather, educators who use their knowledge of intersectionality are prepared to create classrooms and curricular environments that are responsive to the various ways Black students experience school-based anti-Blackness differently.

The violent, ideological notion that the social positioning of Blackness is inferior and less than human is concretized through institutional structures and processes, particularly those grounded in the legacy of slavery—a legacy that presents Blackness as always needing to be contained or punished. As one of society's foremost apparatuses of socialization, US schooling creates and perpetuates harsh punishment practices and largely denies Black students the freedom to exist in schools free of surveillance, making Black education a site of inferior freedom. The pillar of Black fugitive thought details the ways Black educators depart from these anti-Black processes through various methods of escape. To engage Black fugitive thought in practice, educators should fund ways to create spaces of refuge in teaching and learning environments that provide reprieve from the ongoing onslaughts of anti-Blackness. These spaces can be physical (e.g., creating or supporting Black affinity spaces) or curricular (e.g., centering and uplifting Black thought).

Afrofuturism is a core pillar of BLiTE because it shows how Black liberation is oriented toward future ways of living that look radically different from current realities. Afrofuturism is about waiting not for new modes of living to be granted, but for new modes of Black living to be created while fighting against oppressive social contexts. To engage in Black liberation in education is to be informed by past and present ways educational institutions have served Black students, while constantly reimagining actions and structures that will lessen the future impact of anti-Blackness on schooling experiences. Afrofuturism can be used to dispel truths by creating opportunities for students that set them up for future success in ways that prepare them to navigate and overcome the inevitable realities of anti-Blackness they will experience.

Conclusion

Teacher education programs must educate students about the ways anti-Blackness, as it intersects with other forms of oppression, "distort[s] the professional education of teachers, school leaders, and researchers."[27] In order "to generate more accurate and truthful knowledge" about the social realities of schooling in a society organized along hierarchies of race, studying how the Black liberation tradition catalyzes *Black agency* is necessary.[28] For instance, since the 1960s Black students have demonstrated their agency, forging "a change of rising human expectations" by demanding "that both the curriculum and other experiences offered in Black and predominantly white colleges be relevant and meaningful to their needs and to the self-actualization of their potentialities and aspirations."[29]

If public schooling systems are "strongholds of white racism,"[30] educators need to be trained in launching school practices that resist such strongholds. Key to resistance in the Black liberation tradition is *Black consciousness-raising*, or developing an awareness of the external societal structures and ideologies that construct Blackness as less than, while simultaneously developing an awareness of the richness of Black humanity that exists beyond the confines of anti-Blackness.[31] Embedded across all five pillars of BLiTE is providing educators with a framework to commit themselves to understanding the cultivation of raising our students' consciousness around the racial realities that inform our nation's social context in ways that allow them to engage in educational methods committed to truth-telling in the face of violent anti-Black narratives.

CHAPTER 9

Beyond Board Etiquette

Responding to Racism in K–12 School Boardrooms

James Bridgeforth

Media reports of contentious K–12 school board meetings across the United States have become common as board and community members openly grapple with issues of race, racism, equity, and justice in schools. Debates over school resource officers, curricula focused on race and racism, and explicit acts of racism in schools have often developed into crises that filled school board meeting agendas in countless communities. In many cases, recent demonstrations and protests against racial equity and justice at school board meetings have led to critical shifts in policy and practice within districts.[1] While perhaps more visible due to the twenty-four-hour news cycle, it is important to note that these contentious moments, hereafter referred to as racial crises, are not new to K–12 education.

Racial crises, defined as high-stress, time-sensitive incidents of a racialized nature with a high probability of negative implications for racially minoritized people, organizations, or communities, have long plagued communities across the United States. Due to the endemic nature of racism in society, these crises are often predictable manifestations of racial inequities, discrimination, or violence. The historical record detailing manifestations of racism in schools offers numerous examples of such crises unfolding in the boardroom. Whether the crisis has involved racial violence due to desegregation orders,[2] race riots on school property,[3] or continued school closures in predominantly Black and Brown neighborhoods,[4] school boards have long been involved in responses to racial crises. In fact, their actions at times have caused some of these moments of crisis.

Throughout the twentieth century, school boards were regular litigants in court cases aimed at challenging racial segregation in K–12 schools.[5] Even before the turn of the century in the 1899 decision *Cummings v. Richmond County Board of Education*, school board members sought and won the right to deny Black students a high school education by closing the only Black high school for what were described as "economic reasons," and ultimately forcing Black students to cease further education after elementary school. In *Mendez v. Westminster School District of Orange County* (1947), school board members sought to continue their policy of unequal, racially segregated schools, even going so far as to send members of the same family to different schools.

In sum, school boards have historically engaged in tacit white supremacy through decision-making regarding access to equitable resources based on race. This legacy persists today, as board meeting protocols and routines often uphold white supremacist norms and logics (e.g., neutrality, order, civility, and decorum).[6] These protocols and routines operate at the expense of marginalized community members organizing in pursuit of equity and justice.[7] In response to this impasse, this chapter draws on a single case study of one school board's response to a racial crisis to offer actionable recommendations that board members can use to promote community-centered engagement during moments of racial crisis.

A Racial Crisis of Their Own Making: The Case of the Hemlock School Board

Nestled among rolling green hills dotted with small family farms, it's easy to understand why Rachel, a member of the Hemlock School Board (pseudonym), described her first experiences in the city as "idyllic." She explained that she had initially moved to the community from a large, bustling city to raise her children in nature and reap the benefits of living in a smaller, more rural community. After volunteering in her children's schools and becoming more involved in the community, she successfully ran for a seat on the Hemlock School Board. She represented her initial years as a board member as being fairly typical of most school boards, with a focus on managing the district budget and hiring district leadership. However, as the 2020 presidential election unfolded and the summer 2020 movement against racial injustice spread throughout the country, she explained that a significant shift occurred within the board. Just months after the near-unanimous adoption of an antiracism resolution, a local election dramatically altered the balance of power on the school board.

Rachel shared, "We got two new board members that came on very aggressive right out of the gate, like, 'This place is broken and we're here to fix it.'" During one of the first meetings of the Hemlock School Board with its newly constituted four-to-three conservative majority, the board moved to enact an agenda focused on "traditional education" by introducing a ban on Black Lives Matter and LGBTQ+ Pride flags within Hemlock schools. When characterizing the shock of some within the Hemlock community that the new board would introduce this policy so soon after the district adopted its antiracism resolution, she explained, "You know, the wild part is, is that we're not known as an activist community at all. So the idea that our halls were, like, littered with massive amounts of BLM and pride flags was just false. . . . This was from the beginning a manufactured problem. It's not like we had people coming to us in droves saying 'Oh my gosh, this is crazy. It's too much.'" While board meeting records indicate some opposition to the inclusion of these symbols in Hemlock classrooms, meeting minutes and recordings clearly demonstrate that a significant majority of the community members who regularly attended board meetings were in support of the symbols in schools.

At the second board meeting of the year, the Hemlock School Board encountered an energized and mobilized group of community members seeking to comment on the board's potential ban on Black Lives Matter and Pride flags. In total, ninety-one people submitted requests to speak to the board, with twenty-eight participants eventually getting the chance to speak during the first ninety minutes of the board meeting. Like previous public comments concerning the Black Lives Matter signs and Pride flags, most of the speakers (65 percent) were in support of allowing these symbols to remain in Hemlock schools. One speaker presented a support letter signed by all of the district's school counselors while also sharing the stories of marginalized Hemlock students who would be impacted by the potential ban. In contrast, Peter, the vice-chair of the Hemlock School Board, stated, "No one can deny these symbols are divisive and have taken attention away from where they need to be which is teaching the fundamentals of education. Taxpayers pay for schools to teach children how to read and do math, not what to think about personal ideologies. Social justice is not some universal moral imperative that everyone has to agree on." Similarly, another conservative board member utilized her comments to discuss the contentious environment that had developed in the aftermath of the board's actions, describing how "teachers and parents are afraid to speak, kids are being bullied for being straight, and businesses were being attacked." The board chair acknowledged how this issue seemed to have divided the community, noting that the board had received over five hundred emails about this issue alone.

Throughout the next month, the Hemlock School Board continued to hear from community members in support of allowing Black Lives Matter and Pride flags in schools through emails, letters, and statements during board public comment sessions. Despite this significant community support for the symbols, the Hemlock School Board enacted the ban on Black Lives Matter and Pride flags, nominally in service of ending what conservative board members characterized as "divisiveness" within the community. This case provides a useful lens through which we can understand how racialized frames such as divisiveness and a commitment to civility, along with a fealty to traditional hierarchies, influence possibilities for community-centered racial crisis leadership.

Racialized Frames and Hierarchies as Barriers to Racial Crisis Leadership

Wendy Leo Moore explains that certain racialized frames can collectively help to organize the practices and norms of white institutional spaces, which I argue characterize K–12 school boards.[8] One such frame that undergirds the organizing logic of many formal public spaces is the notion of "order." As an organizing frame, "order" can be characterized as a necessary state of being or way of doing something that can maintain institutional goals or hierarchies that are inherently influenced by broader societal structures such as racism or white supremacy. In this way, order has been taken up in racialized ways that historically have been employed to silence or police various forms of protest or dissent.

In his *Letter from a Birmingham Jail*, King critiques white moderates' steadfast commitment to this concept of "order" by juxtaposing their desire for what he calls a negative peace (the absence of tension) to a positive peace (the presence of justice).[9] The newly elected, conservative board chair offered a useful example of the commitment to the absence of tension when he began his tenure by committing to "change, the need for civility, correcting divisiveness in the community and on the board, and setting aside politics to focus on education for every single student." This statement presents an understanding of the role of the board that is grounded in civility, a reliance on traditional hierarchies, and a commitment to apolitical understandings of leadership—none of which have served marginalized and minoritized communities well throughout history.

Several board members described how throughout the contentious process of banning the Black Lives Matter and Pride symbols, their ability to shape and challenge the process was limited due to the board's governance model that relied heavily on norms of respecting the chair as the board leader and spokesperson. One of these board members, Naomi, explained, "I'm hesitant of coming out publicly, because that's not my . . . you know, the board chair is our spokesperson and I [spoke] to a couple of news media during this situation but I'm very careful because I don't feel that's my position." Rachel also struggled with this norm of relying on traditional hierarchies, explaining how her thinking had evolved since the board began its efforts to ban these symbols. She shared, "I refuse to stay silent on these things. You know, you can have board etiquette, which is important, but this is beyond etiquette, right? I mean, this is racism and homophobia and oppression." Reflecting on how the actions of the conservative board majority shaped her practices as a board member, she explained:

> I'd been a member for about four years operating under this principle of "When a decision is made, we all stick together" you know? "We present a united front" to now saying bullshit to that. Like, I'm not going to go along with this because it is hateful and awful and you're literally destroying my kids' schools. Like I see it. It's right before my eyes and I'm not staying silent on that. So, you know, I've gotten some pushback from people who think that it's not professional [air quotes used]. It's been tough but also super rewarding, right? Like, we don't often get platforms to say, "No, I'm taking a stand against this because it's awful." Being able to do that is it's hard, but it's good.

Through these words, Rachel offers a vision of racial crisis leadership at the board level that suggests that traditional norms of board governance may not be suitable for a form of racial crisis leadership that centers the needs of marginalized communities. Rather, if the needs of these communities are to be served, board members may have to engage in behaviors that could be deemed unprofessional or combative but at least have the potential to push back against inequitable or oppressive policies and practices.

Responding to Racial Crises in the Boardroom

Since their inception, school boards have undergone significant reforms to root out corruption and bring about more inclusive, representative forms of governance.[10] However, these ideals have often been slow to materialize in practice, with boards continuing to concentrate power in the hands of elite political actors as they "worked to blunt the demands of the people."[11] While research has demonstrated that "Americans as a whole want school boards who listen and engage with parents and stakeholders to be in charge of local public schools," the reality remains that this community-engaged approach to board leadership is often elusive for marginalized communities.[12] The following recommendations seek to shift board practice toward the promise of meaningful board engagement and possibilities for racial redress during moments of racial crisis.

Rejecting Respectability and the Specter of Divisiveness

Discursive strategies of policing protests and community organizing through critiques grounded in norms of civility and decorum have long been utilized to dismiss marginalized communities' valid concerns.[13] Returning to King's framing of a negative peace (the absence of tension) and a positive peace (the presence of justice), the specter of divisiveness can encourage board members to be more beholden to a politics of peace over progress. This frame of political leadership prioritizes peace and community cohesion, even when one's actions enact real harm to others within the community. This belief prioritizes a negative peace and sense of commonality over the recognition that differences of opinion are not simply an exercise in reasoned debate. Instead, they reflect a series of policy choices that while perhaps promoting a negative peace, also have profound negative implications for the lives and experiences of marginalized communities.

By focusing on the "divisiveness" of community outrage rather than the substantive ideas of what communities are advocating for, elite political actors (e.g., school board members) can continue to enact and uphold inequitable policies in service of a veneer of unity. While not intended to advocate for the full dissolution of civility in the boardroom, Rachel's willingness to challenge board etiquette and traditional hierarchies should serve as a model for community-centered racial crisis leadership. If racially equitable and just experiences for marginalized students are the intended outcomes for their students, board members must be willing to reject the specter of divisiveness and use their positional authority to challenge traditional hierarchies and speak out against oppressive policies. For example, if members are serving in the political minority, they might consider how they wield procedural tools to their advantage to delay the policy development process while simultaneously building external coalitions of community stakeholders. Board members' commitments to collegiality cannot outweigh their commitment to the communities that they serve.

Developing Board-Level Racial Literacy

State-level professional development requirements for board members are often varied, and training sessions are largely aimed at promoting better relationships with superintendents, along with learning how to navigate legal and fiscal issues that the board will have to address.[14] While these issues are undoubtedly important in learning how to be an effective board member, it is also important that states consider how school boards have more recently become contentious sites of racialized public engagement through heightened awareness of the policymaking aspect of school board governance. Whereas board members may have previously been able to navigate their initial experiences on the board without much additional support or training, the realities of board service today may require additional skills and capacities in order to effectively navigate any number of crises that may emerge during their time on the board.

Professional associations responsible for board member learning and development should consider developing a curriculum that directly addresses how to increase racial literacy development for new and currently serving board members. This draft curriculum could be adapted to each state's particular context and needs but should unequivocally be grounded in ensuring that board members have a strong, shared understanding of (1) the myriad forms of racism, (2) how racism, white supremacy, and anti-Blackness are embedded in education policy and practice, and (3) concrete ways in which they might use their positional authority as board members to disrupt and dismantle racially unjust policies and practices in service of mitigating racialized harms for racially minoritized communities.

Interrogating Board Routines and Norms

Rather than functioning as spaces for democratic deliberation and representative democracy, school boards continue to use their rules and policies in an attempt to diminish marginalized community members' ability to speak, "wield[ing] the rules in inconsistent ways that shifted over time, thereby maintaining whiteness as property."[15] This pattern of racialized censorship can persist even when school boards comprise people of color.[16] Therefore, it is critical that meaningful changes in board-level racial crisis leadership must go beyond the symbolic (e.g., increased racial representation on boards) to prioritize reshaping boardroom policies and practices. To facilitate these changes, board leadership should employ regular, comprehensive audits of board routines and the norms that shape their implementation.

Prior to the start of each academic year, board members often engage in planning workshops where they establish board goals for the coming year. This is an opportune time for critical reflection on *how* board members engage with their constituencies, *which* constituencies are most often engaged, and *whether* community engagement practices demonstrably shape the policy development process. Board leaders should also consider how their engagement policies influence who regularly accesses engagement opportunities. In reviewing these policies, they might consider how such policies are aligned with stated goals. These reflective practices have the potential to impact structural change within the boardroom by shining a light on taken-for-granted norms and routines that may regularly exclude marginalized communities.

CHAPTER 10

Shared Equity Leadership

A Strategy for Saving DEI Efforts at Colleges and Universities

Adrianna Kezar and Elizabeth Holcombe

Less than three years after the murder of George Floyd and the subsequent protests against racism in all aspects of American life, a significant backlash against diversity, equity, and inclusion (DEI) efforts is already in full force. Numerous state legislatures are now asking college and university campuses to report on their budgets devoted to DEI efforts, as well as to provide lists of the programs, trainings, services, and efforts focused on DEI as they prepare to identify and cut such efforts. Florida has become the poster child for leading this conservative backlash against DEI, but several other state legislatures, including North Carolina, North Dakota, Texas, and Tennessee, have passed laws aimed at dismantling DEI efforts, with proposed bills in many other states across the country.[1] The Manhattan Institute, a conservative think tank, has developed model legislation that was quickly promoted by lawmakers in several states that would abolish DEI offices and staff, eliminate the use of diversity statements in hiring, and bar trainings that educate staff and faculty on how to identify and fight against systemic racism.[2]

One of the main reasons why DEI efforts are particularly vulnerable on campuses across the country is that they have not become a normative practice ingrained within campus culture. Typically, DEI efforts in higher education are isolated or siloed to a chief diversity officer (CDO) or DEI office that often exist outside the mainstream work of campus. DEI efforts are more easily under threat and vulnerable to attacks when they remain outside our normal ways of conducting business. Separate DEI positions or offices are easy to identify and have become easy targets for political attacks from conservative politicians.

In recent studies conducted by the University of Southern California's (USC) Pullias Center for Higher Education, which focuses on campuses that have made progress on eliminating equity gaps and advancing their DEI agendas, our research team identified shared equity leadership (SEL) as an approach that deeply embeds DEI into day-to-day campus operations and drives culture change.[3] Campuses that used SEL became much more diverse in terms of hiring, promotion, and retention of faculty and staff from diverse racial backgrounds. And the campus leaders dismantled problematic policies and practices that have stood in the way of equity. In SEL environments, equity becomes everyone's work and not only the work of a CDO or DEI office. By becoming embedded in faculty, administrative, and staff roles across campus, the work is less of a target for cuts. Not only does this approach shield DEI from cuts, but it also ensures that the work has the critical mass of human resources necessary to truly transform institutions into the equitable and inclusive spaces we hope they can be. SEL offers the organizational structures to broadly distribute work and provides the planning and accountability apparatus so that the work is sustained over time, even as it is distributed among many more people.

Can SEL fully shield DEI from attacks? Not completely, as we see from bans on critical race theory, which suggest that DEI-related practices and ideas can also be targeted in addition to organizational structures.[4] Nonetheless, adopting SEL would certainly make it much more difficult for legislatures to locate and isolate the work for broad-scale cuts and bans. And if equity-oriented work is routinized more as a good practice, such as disaggregating data to look for equity gaps, it would be much harder to see the activity as problematic given that it is hard to grab headlines for following sound administrative practice.

In this chapter we review the characteristics of SEL and describe how it can address the current political moment and help maintain DEI efforts. We end by suggesting ways to organize DEI efforts using an SEL approach, both in states where DEI is under attack and in those states not facing political challenges to the work.

What Is Shared Equity Leadership?

SEL emerged from our recent research of leaders at eight colleges and universities in the United States who were successfully advancing their DEI goals. Conducted by the American Council on Education (ACE) and USC's Pullias Center, the idea for the study originated from the broader question of why campuses have generally made so little progress on DEI goals in the past forty years, as reflected in ACE's 2019 analysis of racial equity outcomes across students, staff, and faculty.[5] The research team wanted to identify campuses that were bucking this trend and actually making progress on closing equity gaps and other DEI goals. We wondered, were there common characteristics of leadership and organization at such institutions that we could identify to help other campuses advance equity? What types of approaches would allow leaders to truly make progress toward culture change that embeds DEI goals within the fabric of the institution? Our study found that campuses that *had* made substantial progress on their DEI goals—despite their institutional type and context differences—shared a collaborative approach that we refer to as shared equity leadership (SEL).

SEL is a leadership approach that scales DEI work and creates culture change by connecting personal and organizational transformation. We define "leadership" in a nonpositional way that includes faculty, staff, students, and community members, in addition to senior administrators. SEL creates a critical mass of faculty, staff, and administrators who are all committed to the work, capable of leading the work, and supported through institutional processes, policies, and structures. The goal of SEL is to create culture change that embeds shared values around DEI into the core of an organization. SEL is a collaborative process where leaders across campus work together, contributing to a change in organizational culture in which equity becomes everyone's work rather than being siloed in a single office or within a single leader's purview.

As noted above, SEL involves personal and organizational transformation, which are both essential for promoting lasting cultural change. Personal transformation involves the process of individuals understanding the structural nature of inequity, deepening their own personal commitment to equity, and taking actions to create changes. By organizational transformation, we mean that an organization transforms its long-existing norms, structures, processes, practices, and policies that privilege certain groups over others and maintain the inequitable status quo. New structures that center equity help instantiate new norms and values across the organization. Personal and organizational transformation reinforce each other. As more leaders grow to be equity-minded and learn to work collectively, the force for change toward equity increases, which drives organizational transformation. As organizations transform to establish new policies and practices that support equity work, individuals gain more resources and opportunities to increase their understanding of systemic inequity, develop the capacity to create change, and feel supported to do equity work.

The SEL model (figure 10.1) entails three main elements: (1) a *personal journey toward critical consciousness* in which leaders solidify their commitment to equity, (2) a set of *values* that center equity and guide the work, and (3) a set of *practices* that leaders enact collectively to change inequitable structures.[6] There are nine values and seventeen practices. However, every individual does not have to have every value and practice. In fact, among the leaders we interviewed, only a few possessed skills in all areas. Rather, we want to bring a range of expertise or skills from diverse individuals by distributing leadership throughout an organization. With a wider range of skills,

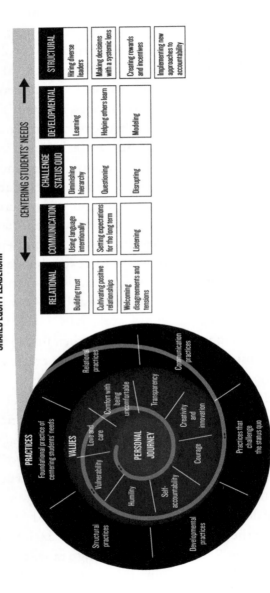

Figure 10.1 Shared equity leadership model

experiences, knowledge, and perspectives, we can enact more of the SEL values and practices, which can create broader and deeper organizational change. In the following sections, we explore each element of the SEL model in greater detail.

Personal Journey Toward Critical Consciousness

At the heart of SEL is the notion that leaders must first turn inward and do their own personal work in order to then turn outward to transform their institutions—this is what we call the *personal journey toward critical consciousness.* In this process, leaders reflect on their own identities and experiences, as well as the broader structural and systemic nature of inequities and how they fit within those systems and structures. Personal work means examining one's understanding of white supremacy, privilege, oppression, and systemic racism and other "isms." Engaging in the personal journey helps make the work authentic due to one's growing compassion and empathy related to these issues. With that realization, DEI issues become personal, and leaders develop a greater sense of responsibility and commitment to creating a new and equitable structure.

In many DEI efforts to date, it has been left up to individual discretion whether to opt into personal development work. And now in today's environment, even offering trainings that would contribute to individual development around DEI issues is decried as indoctrination by conservative opponents.[7] The SEL model both differs from previous efforts that were dependent on individual buy-in and can avoid the danger of being labeled as an indoctrination effort. In SEL environments, a network of leaders collaborate to foster individual growth and development, eliminating the need for individuals to opt in and bear sole responsibility for their learning. The personal journey approach also differs from traditional DEI workshops that focus on topics like implicit bias or microaggressions. Personal journey development focuses on enhancing leaders' understanding of their own identities and the systems or structures they are working within, rather than directly addressing DEI topics. This work equips leaders to act authentically and promote equity without necessarily being labeled as DEI training. Nevertheless, adjustments in language or framing of particular opportunities may be necessary in many states. For example, leaders in politically conservative states may want to refer to just "personal journey" rather than the full name of "personal journey toward critical consciousness," given the potential association of "critical consciousness" with critical race theory.

Our research points to several different avenues to aid leaders in their personal journey. Individual modeling and mentoring is one strategy, wherein a leader takes another person under their wing, posing questions and recounting their own journey. Another approach to personal journey work is forming collective groups such as book clubs or learning communities that are ongoing in order to support personal journey work. Both of these approaches fall outside the traditional definition of "trainings" that have currently been targeted. It is more difficult for opponents to target an approach like mentoring or book clubs.

Values

The second element of the SEL model is *values*, which are the beliefs and ideals shared among leaders across campus. The values represent a way of being, showing up, and relating to others as a leader. Individual leaders learn to embody the values of SEL through their personal journey work as well as through working with others who model the values. Some of the SEL values may look familiar from other approaches to leadership, such as courage or creativity. However, many SEL values differ and emphasize collaborative and relational processes, such as transparency and comfort with being uncomfortable. They also delve into personal and emotional aspects of leadership, such as love and care, humility, and vulnerability. Table 10.1 provides detailed descriptions of all nine SEL values. These values are essential to creating culture change as they establish an environment in which people develop trust and safety to transform their daily practice. SEL values are not something that political leaders can easily attack—they are not tangible like budgets, trainings, or programs. And the values themselves are hard to make an argument against in terms of being important for fostering a supportive campus environment.

SEL *practices* represent new ways of acting that are oriented toward challenging inequities and creating new structures and policies. We define practices as the ongoing, regular activities that leaders perform both individually and collectively to advance a DEI agenda. We identified sixteen practices and categorized them into six domains: the fundamental practice of centering the needs of systematically marginalized communities, relational practices, communication practices, developmental practices, practices challenging the status quo, and structural practices. Relational and communication practices suggest effective ways of working with others and across differences. Developmental practices build knowledge and skills, fostering individuals' ability to engage in equity

Table 10.1 Description of SEL values

Love and care	Leaders feel and display love and care for those with and for whom they are working. They approach any relationship with a deep sense of caring and compassion, even if they disagree or have had contrasting experiences.
Comfort with being uncomfortable	Equity work sometimes requires leaders to sit with the emotions and pains of others—even when uncomfortable—rather than immediately jumping to finding solutions. It is important for leaders to be comfortable with such feelings of discomfort.
Transparency	Transparency means that leaders are honest, clear, and open about decision-making, successes, failures, and challenges of their work.
Creativity and imagination	Creativity and imagination are necessary because there are no universally agreed-upon ways of doing equity work and leaders must imagine new possibilities.
Courage	Courage means standing up for equity even when it's not popular or easy and remaining dedicated in the face of resistance or skepticism.
Accountability to self and others	Leaders must hold themselves accountable for doing the work, getting results, learning about equity, challenging their preconceived notions, and being willing to change their beliefs and practices as they continue to learn and grow. Leaders must also be accountable to one another and the community for doing the work.
Humility	Humility means admitting when one has done something wrong or when something has not worked well. Leaders understand that they do not have all the answers or solutions, their experience isn't everyone's experience, and they have things to learn from other people.
Vulnerability	Vulnerability means being able to be open about difficult personal experiences or being willing to risk exposing one's true self, even without knowing exactly how that will be received. Being vulnerable helps leaders build connections, trust one another, and better understand others' perspectives and experiences.
Mutuality	Mutuality underpins all the other SEL values, emphasizing a shift away from traditional egoistic notions of leadership focused on the individual leader and instead embracing notions of leadership as a reciprocal and collective process.

work. Practices that challenge the status quo encourage leaders to call out the entrenched policies and practices that reproduce inequities, while actively working to dismantle them. Structural practices support leaders to implement concrete changes to organizational structures and culture. Table 10.2 presents all of the SEL practices.[8]

While most SEL practices are not likely to be targeted by conservative opponents of DEI work, a few may need to be modified to withstand political scrutiny. Providing rewards or incentives for engaging in DEI work and allocating budgets to units that meet DEI goals are probably the three biggest lightning rod practices that will need reconsideration in the SEL model in conservative states. While these important practices demonstrate the value of DEI through the tangible allocation of resources, we have seen that budget allocations for centralized offices of DEI work are under attack.[9] It is unclear whether DEI funding operating in more decentralized spaces will also come under attack, but it is reasonable to suspect it will. Reward systems are very visible, so changing promotion and tenure processes to support DEI goals, for example, is likely untenable in conservative states. We think that leaders should use their creativity to consider other ways to maintain diversity in hiring and prioritize DEI goals in the face of possible restrictions of incentive and budgeting systems in the near term.

Organizing DEI Work in SEL Environments

It is critical to note that CDOs and central DEI offices were present at most of the SEL campuses we studied, at first as a catalytic agent and then as a hub to connect and coordinate the shared and distributed SEL work. However, we also

Table 10.2 SEL practices

Foundational practice	Relational practices	Communication practices	Developmental practices	Practices that challenge the status quo	Structural practices
Understanding and centering students' needs	Building trust	Using language intentionally	Learning	Diminishing hierarchy	Hiring diverse leaders (or composing diverse teams)
	Cultivating positive relationships	Setting expectations	Helping others learn	Questioning	Systemic decision-making
	Welcoming disagreements and tensions	Listening	Modeling	Disrupting	Creating rewards and incentives
					Implementing new approaches to accountability

found that some campuses used the president's cabinet, a task force, or council instead of a central DEI office to coordinate their culture-changing work. What is promising about SEL in today's environment is that it provides alternative models for continuing the goals of DEI when centralized DEI offices are made politically infeasible or even illegal. A campus can repurpose an existing structure or office to serve as a coordinating unit to keep culture change sustained and continue to work toward their equity goals, even in today's challenging political climate. Over time, many campuses in our study found that as they decentralized the work of DEI, the need for a central hub or coordinating office diminished. However, these structural changes take time, and campuses responding to threats to shut down their DEI central offices cannot possibly distribute the work quickly enough to meet the demands of politicians and effectively maintain their progress.

Our body of work on SEL provides a blueprint for campuses aspiring to transition from a siloed DEI structure to a shared approach, with information about organizational structures, accountability, alteration of roles, job descriptions, capacity building, and other key information.[10] Yet it takes significant time to plan the move from a centralized structure to a new one. It does not happen in days, weeks, or even months. The campuses we studied who moved to SEL approaches did so over the course of years. It is possible that today's challenging political environment could create a sense of urgency to move toward SEL more quickly, but we doubt this could happen without, at minimum, eight to twelve months of planning, even when accelerated.

Central DEI offices remain strong anchors for the work, and leaders should try to keep such offices in states where this is possible. In addition, leaders should recommit to the original goals of these offices to create culture change.[11] President and provosts in states that are not under attack should use this moment to examine their DEI strategy and see how they can empower DEI central offices to work to embed the work more effectively across campuses. SEL is one approach they should consider to help with that embedding. In states where central DEI offices are prohibited or under attack, we offer up SEL as an approach to continue making progress on DEI goals in spite of such attacks. An SEL approach does not preclude advocating for a return of DEI-specific positions and offices, but it does allow for continuation of the work in the meantime. Given the pressures that colleagues in many states are already facing, now is a good time to begin conversations and planning toward SEL to ensure that this important work can continue regardless of political headwinds.

CHAPTER 11

Critically Engaging the Regressive Racial Backlash Reform Movement in Higher Education

Jarrett T. Gupton

The Black Lives Matter movement of 2020 created a racial reckoning that forced the United States and its higher education institutions to examine their complicity with structural racism. Although the movement led to increased training, teaching, and discussions about racial equity and dismantling systemic racism, our nation subsequently responded with resentment.[1] That resentment transformed into a regressive education reform policy movement aimed at enshrining colorblind meritocracy and erasing curriculum, theories, and discussion of race in colleges and universities. This chapter reviews the chronological evolution of regressive racial backlash policies targeting higher education and presents the four rhetoric arcs that have framed the regressive movement. The chapter concludes with recommendations for higher education administrators, faculty, and community members to critically engage and push forward racial equity agendas in response to regressive policy efforts.

Chronology of Regressive Backlash
2020: Divisive Concepts

The regressive racial policy backlash started in the fall of 2020 when then-President Trump issued Executive Order (EO) 13950, Combating Race and Sex Stereotyping, which banned the federal government and its contractors from conducting racial diversity training.[2] EO 13950 portrayed discussions of structural inequality as a threat to American democracy as a colorblind meritocracy.

> Today, however, many people are pushing a different vision of America that is grounded in hierarchies based on collective social and political identities rather than in the inherent and equal dignity of every person as an individual. This ideology is rooted in the pernicious and false belief that America is an irredeemably racist and sexist country; that some people, simply on account of their race or sex, are oppressors; and that racial and sexual identities are more important than our common status as human beings and Americans.[3]

Although EO 13950 made reference to a pernicious ideology, it never explicitly stated what ideology it was referencing, only that it is destructive, malign, and "is now migrating from the fringes of American society and threatens to infect core institutions of our country."[4] EO 13950 prohibited the promotion of stereotyping or scapegoating based on race or sex; further, it disallowed any organizations receiving federal grants from indoctrinating employees with views related to "divisive concepts" that undermine the idea of the US as a colorblind meritocracy. EO 13950 defined divisive concepts as:

- One race or sex is inherently superior to another race or sex;
- The United States is fundamentally racist or sexist;
- An individual, by virtue of his or her race or sex, is inherently racist, sexist, or oppressive, whether consciously or unconsciously;
- An individual should be discriminated against or receive adverse treatment solely or partly because of his or her race or sex;
- Members of one race or sex cannot and should not attempt to treat others without respect for race or sex;
- An individual's moral character is necessarily determined by his or her race or sex;
- An individual, by virtue of his or her race or sex, bears responsibility for actions committed in the past by other members of the same race or sex;
- Any individual should feel discomfort, guilt, anguish, or any other form of psychological distress on account of his or her race or sex; and
- Meritocracy or traits such as a hard work ethic are racist or sexist or created by a particular race to oppress another.[5]

EO 13950 had an immediate impact on higher education institutions. In September 2020, the Justice Department investigated Princeton University for its acknowledgment and effort to redress the school's history of structural racism.[6] In October, the US Justice Department sued Yale University for allegedly violating the Civil Rights Act of 1964, claiming the school had discriminated against white and Asian American applicants in the admissions process.[7] EO 13950 also had a chilling effect on public institutions, such as the University of Iowa, halting diversity and equity–related training for fear they would lose federal research grants.[8] EO 13950 effectively placed a gag order on many colleges and universities by prohibiting courses, training, and speakers under threat of instigation and loss of funding.[9] Although President Biden revoked the EO 13950 in January 2021, it was the template for the onslaught of regressive political backlash legislation.

2021: Anti–Critical Race Theory and Indoctrination

With the revocation of EO 13950, regressive politicians at the state and federal levels began to recast their arguments. Early in 2021, regressive policymakers targeted critical race theory (CRT) as an example of what EO 13950 defined as a divisive concept being taught in schools.[10] Following the murder of George Floyd and Black Lives Matter protests, schools and universities witnessed an increase in antiracism curriculum and training. Regressive politicians created a warped narrative that suggested that the teaching of CRT in schools was overemphasizing issues of systemic racial inequality, causing white students to feel discomfort and guilt and diminishing their sense of patriotism. Materials that endorsed antiracism or the

1619 Project were also labeled as divisive concepts. Although CRT is an intersectional theoretical and practical framework that critiques how various social structures (legal, political, cultural, and economic) contribute to historic and pervasive racial inequities, conservatives invoked the name CRT as a central narrative in regressive racial backlash legislation; they have offered misguided and bad-faith interpretations of the theory[11] to create a manufactured crisis. The end result of that artificial panic was several states passing anti-CRT or divisive concept laws that were carbon copies of EO 13950 aimed at schools and colleges. Roughly ten states (Alabama, Idaho, Iowa, Montana, New Hampshire, North Dakota, Oklahoma, Tennessee, Texas, and Utah) passed legislative measures that limited what educators could say about race and what materials they could use to teach about race and US history.

In addition to anti-CRT legislation, regressive politicians also began making claims that colleges and universities were sites of liberal indoctrination and restricting intellectual freedom on campuses. The state of Florida was one of the more vocal advocates, passing a policy to survey and monitor freedom of political expression on campuses among students, staff, and faculty. In 2021 the Florida legislature proposed and passed the Intellectual Freedom and Viewpoint Diversity Act, or House Bill 233 (HB 233). While expressing support for HB 233 to the Florida Board of Governors, Florida House Speaker Chris Sprowls, Republican, warned of colleges catering to the woke mob,[12] and Florida Senate President Wilton Simpson claimed that universities in Florida were socialist factories.[13] In signing HB 233 into law, Florida Governor Ron DeSantis remarked, "It used to be thought that a university campus was a place where you would be exposed to a lot of different ideas . . . [u]nfortunately now, the norm is really [that] you have orthodoxies that are promoted, and other viewpoints are shunned or even suppressed. We don't want that in Florida."[14]

Florida's Intellectual Freedom and Viewpoint Diversity bill has three provisions. First, HB 233 requires the State Board of Education and the Board of Governors to conduct an annual viewpoint diversity survey and assessment of intellectual freedom among higher education students, staff, and faculty within the state's public colleges and universities. Although described as objective, nonpartisan, and statistically valid, the survey is "to ensure that Florida's postsecondary students' will be shown diverse ideas and opinions, including those that they may disagree with or find uncomfortable."[15] Second, HB 233 removes the need for instructor consent to record lectures for educational purposes.[16] Finally, legislation stipulates that colleges and universities may not "shield" or limit access to ideas that students, staff, or faculty may find uncomfortable or offensive.[17]

Florida was not the only state to pass intellectual freedom legislation as part of the backlash to racial equity. The University System of Georgia produced a 102-page report (including data for all 26 campuses) after State Representative Emory Dunahoo expressed concern over the teaching of privilege and oppression.[18] At the behest of the state legislature, the Iowa Board of Regents is requiring a statement on all syllabi that endorses free speech and debate of ideas and that "students will not be penalized for the content or viewpoints of their speech as long as student expression in a class context is germane to the subject matter of the class and conveyed in an appropriate manner."[19] Further, Tennessee, Montana, and Idaho have introduced or enacted intellectual diversity and free speech bills. The purpose of these bills is state-sponsored surveillance of college classrooms. The proliferation of anti-CRT legislation has effectively muted the conversation on racial equity in schools and colleges in certain states.

2022: Stop Woke

In 2022, the regressive backlash against racial equity made a linguistic pivot. On December 15, 2021, Florida Governor Ron DeSantis introduced the Stop WOKE (Wrongs to Our Kids and Employees) Act, saying, "In Florida, we are taking a stand against the state-sanctioned racism that is critical race theory."[20] The Stop WOKE Act is a carbon copy of EO 13950. The bill enumerates eight of the nine provisions in EO 13950. It limits training on diversity, equity, and inclusion (DEI) and prohibits the teaching of divisive concepts (e.g., critical race theory, the 1619 Project, systemic inequality) unless presented among other theories objectively and without endorsement.[21] Moreover, the bill prohibits content or instruction that requires an individual to feel discomfort, psychological distress, guilt, anguish, or shame due to the past actions of members of the same race, ethnicity, sex, or national origin.[22]

In addition, the Stop WOKE Act introduces the concept of woke ideology, which has become a rallying cry for regressive politicians. While previous legislation was focused on race and theories like CRT, woke ideology seems to include all discussions of systemic inequality related to race, gender, and sexual orientation. Legislation targeting divisive concepts in education has weaponized boards of education for both K–12 and higher education, granting them latitude to punish and retaliate against individuals for including racial justice and systemic inequality in their teaching, training, or research.

The year 2022 witnessed regressive politicians continuing their assault on racial equity in education. In November of 2022, a US District Court judge, Mark Walker, ruled Florida's Stop Woke Act law unconstitutional, saying it violated the First Amendment and was impermissibly vague.[23] In addition, Judge Walker stated, "If Florida truly believes we live in a post-racial society, then let it make its case. . . . But it cannot win the argument by muzzling its opponents."[24] Although the state of Florida has appealed the ruling, the law remains under court injunction. While the regressive rhetoric has pivoted toward the language of woke ideology, the endgame is still silencing all discussions of racial equity in P-20 education in favor of colorblind meritocracy.

2023: Anti–Diversity, Equity, and Inclusion

While the legislative measures related to divisive concepts represent the initial waves of regressive reform, the next wave of racial equity backlash legislation is winding its way through legislative committees. Regressive politicians are now targeting institutional autonomy along with diversity, equity, and inclusion initiatives. For example, Florida, with HB 999 and Senate Bill (SB) 266, allows the board to review mission statements, programs, and curricula that are "based on theories that systemic racism, sexism, oppression, or privilege are inherent in the institutions of the United States and were created to maintain social, political, or economic inequities."[25] Furthermore, HB 999 prohibits race and gender studies courses from being included as part of the general education curriculum.

Instead, HB 999 requires that all humanities-related courses "must afford students the ability to think critically through mastering subjects concerned with human culture, especially literature, history, art, music, and philosophy, and must include sections from the Western Canon."[26] Anti-DEI legislation, like HB 999, continues to constrict the discussion of racial equity in favor of white European Westernized philosophy. Ohio's SB 83 is structured similarly to HB 999, but it includes an institutional neutrality clause prohibiting colleges and universities from adopting a position on contemporary controversial topics. Institutional neutrality threatens racial equity, as it silences colleges and universities from stating their support of social justice and racial equity. While Florida was the first state to pass anti-DEI legislation, the states of Arizona, Iowa, Missouri, Ohio, Oklahoma, and Texas still have anti-DEI bills pending.

Over the last three years, conservatives have advanced a regressive education reform policy agenda that aims to silence the discussion of racial equity and social justice The national backlash to silence the discussion of structural inequality is not only a means to remove specific pedagogies, epistemologies, or methodologies; rather, it is a strategic campaign to erase the histories, realities, and presence of indigenous, minoritized, or marginalized individuals. The regressive backlash that started with EO 13950 has morphed into a regressive education reform movement bent on abolishing all means of addressing racial and systemic inequality and cementing the US as a colorblind meritocracy.

Recommendations for Responding to the Regressive Backlash

The chronology of the evolution of regressive backlash policies presented in this chapter presents a myriad of challenges for educators and campus leaders. In light of the regressive policy wave, faculty, staff, and administrators should practice three specific forms of critical engagement (self, organizational, and communal). Critical engagement is acknowledging the existence of historic and pervasive structural inequality (based on a myriad of socially constructed factors) and the role of various forms of power in maintaining those systems of inequity. Further, it means consciously making choices that dismantle those inequitable structures to establish and sustain equitable systems, structures, and outcomes for all. Critical engagement promotes transformative change and requires integration throughout the organizational structure or social system.

First, critical self-engagement is an honest and rigorous reflexive practice that confronts biases and how we are implicated in systems of inequality and oppression. If racial equity is something educators and leaders value, then practicing critical self-engagement and honest reflexivity helps embed that value into their everyday actions and practices. Critical self-engagement requires an examination of pedagogy, outcomes, and actions to ensure that they are in alignment with the value of racial equity. It is important to remember that multicultural competence is a continual process of honest reflexivity. Critical self-engagement creates accountability in expanding our capacity for multicultural competence.

The next form of critical engagement is organizational. Critical organizational engagement requires intense and thoughtful examination of the mission, goals, and institutional metrics to ensure alignment with and progress toward racial equity. If schools and universities strive for racial equity, then they must reconcile any inequity in accessibility, affordability, inclusion, and outcomes. In that sense, critical organizational engagement demands and creates institutional accountability. Schools and colleges cannot have missions that endorse racial equity and outcomes that reflect racial inequality. The challenge is to thoroughly examine institutional policies and practices and align them with equity for all students.

The third area of critical engagement is communal. Critical community engagement helps amplify the public mission of schools and universities. It allows the public to take part in the process and demonstrates the value of teaching and research. Critical engagement involves a level of reciprocity with the multiple communities that are linked to the organization. Giving access and power to the community makes it easier to advocate among various political arenas, shape the organizational culture, and help individual educators and leaders continue the process of building multicultural competence. Moreover, critical community engagement is political, as it is not neutral on its stance toward racial equity.

Educators, administrators, students, and families must make their expertise and realities heard at the local, state, and federal levels. Further, they must work in collaboration with lobbyists, unions, and community groups to strategically craft, position, and drive forward a racial equity-focused legislative agenda. In the face of a retaliatory regressive educational reform movement, educators need community support to stand by their practical knowledge and personal conviction and teach about race and racism. Critical community engagement is not only about the research mission: it is also about the responsibility to the public to speak the truth about a misguided ideology like colorblind meritocracy.

Conclusion

The regressive policy backlash against the murder of George Floyd and the Black Lives Matter movement has created a fabricated panic around schools and universities advancing racial equity in the US. The backlash to the push for racial justice reflects a selfish and self-absorbed neoliberal antiracist frame that presents a warped and misshapen concept of racial equity veiled in co-opted language. The regressive racial backlash education reform policies obscure what the Black Lives Matter movement made clear: people want racial justice. The aspirations of a democratic society rooted in racial domination cannot be achieved through colorblind meritocracy. Racial equity in P-20 education requires the hard labor of critical engagement to create the transformative change to dismantle inequitable oppressive systems and establish emancipatory and equitable structures. If P-20 education organizations believe racial equity is something to strive for, they must push forward and critically engage in its promotion and defense.

CHAPTER 12

Anticipated Consequences of "The Big Lie" About Race in America's Schools

Shaun R. Harper

Bans on teaching the truth about our nation's racial past and present are scoring big political wins for governors, state legislators, and school board members. "The Big Lie" will help some get reelected and poise a few others for ascension to higher positions of public service. Meanwhile, millions of Americans will be left to pick up the pieces. It will take years, perhaps decades, to undo the harm manufactured by the recent unfounded attacks on critical race theory; the outlawing of books centering racial topics and racially diverse authors; bans on the inclusion of diversity, equity, and inclusion (DEI) in professional learning experiences for educators and school leaders; and intimidating threats to fire or otherwise penalize educators who responsibly engage racial topics in their classrooms and curricula. In this chapter, I highlight several probable consequences of these and other efforts to suppress truth-teaching. To be sure, what I describe here are not the only negative outcomes that are likely to ensue. It will take years to fully account for the damage "The Big Lie" is doing to our democracy, its citizens, and America's educational institutions.

Our Democracy Will Never Reach Its Full Potential

Freedom. Liberty and justice for all. Equal protection under the law. These and other values are supposedly available to every citizen of the United States of America. But they are not and never have been. The Three-Fifths Compromise, which effectively deemed Black people three-fifths human, denied democracy of reaching its full potential. So too did land theft, colonization, the attempted genocide of Indigenous peoples, over four hundred years of slavery, *Plessy v. Ferguson*'s failed promise of separate but equal schooling, exclusionary college admissions practices, Jim Crow segregation, redlining and discriminatory housing practices, and the modern-day persistence of racial segregation in K–12 educational institutions. Without learning in school that these and other racialized miscarriages of justice occurred in American history, miseducated students will become miseducated adults who do too little to redress centuries of racial problems in our nation. The absence of remedies will cyclically reproduce cultures, structures, and systems that contradict what patriots say America ought to be.

In his book, *Silent Covenants: Brown v. Board of Education and the Unfulfilled Hopes for Racial Reform*, Derrick Bell noted that threats to America's reputation overseas helped accelerate the integration of our nation's K–12 schools.[1] Accordingly, Black American soldiers who were fighting to preserve and export democracy through selfless, sacrificial military service in other parts of the world refused to return to a country where they and their families would continue to be treated as second-class citizens. Bell also highlighted the pressure that was placed on the federal government to deal with America's contradictions. That is, democracy was being exported to other nations across the globe, yet there was too much evidence to confirm that it remained far from realized on US soil, including in its racially segregated schools. The same racism that undermined our democracy then undermines it now. A new generation of miseducated citizens who know nothing or too little about our nation's hypocritical relationship with democratic ideals are guaranteed complicity in failing to realize those values.

Racial Inequities Will Increase in Every Profession and All Facets of Our Society

In most states, laws stipulate that American children must attend school until they are sixteen years old.[2] This means that every American citizen in every community has some level of formal education, even those who dropped out prior to completing high school. These citizens live in communities throughout the nation. They comprise our workforce. Millions annually go to college, some others continue on to law school, medical school, and other graduate degree programs. In just about every industry, college-educated Americans comprise the overwhelming majority of professionals who occupy positions of management and leadership.

In its November 2023 demographic report, the Congressional Research Service notes the following: "As has been true in recent Congresses, the vast majority of Members (93.8% of House Members and 99% of Senators) at the beginning of the 118th Congress have earned at least a bachelor's degree. Sixty-four percent of House Members and 79% of Senators hold educational degrees beyond a bachelor's."[3] According to that same demographic report, more than 70 percent of congresspersons are white. These are the people elected to make policies that affect the lives of every American. Doing so without sufficient prior opportunities to learn about the ways that racism and racist policies have and continue to ruin the lives of people of color will surely lead to the creation of additional racist policies that ruin the lives of people of color.

Professionals often inherit workplaces that have long excluded or neglected people of color. Numerous persistent and pervasive racial inequities require their leadership. The suppression of truth-teaching about race and racism in K–12 schools and higher education institutions will deny professionals the consciousness, knowledge, tools, and skills required to fix longstanding racial problems. Racism will surely worsen under the leadership of miseducated citizens who do not know what it is, let alone how to eradicate it through laws, policies, and practices.

Global Relationships Will Be Compromised

Meaningful, prolonged, and repeated exposure to other people's lived experiences helps reduce stereotypes about those persons and the identity groups in which those persons hold membership.[4] A curriculum that denies students opportunities to substantively engage with a diversity of races, cultures, and histories will deprive them of opportunities to develop mindfulness about stereotypes. Most will also grow up lacking appreciation for cultures that are different from their own. This will ultimately be bad for business. As corporate relationships become more global, partners and clients in other nations will have little patience for miseducated Americans who only understand and appreciate white, Eurocentric cultures. Africa, Asia, and Latin America, for example, are ethnically diverse places. Whites are not the majority in those contexts. If teaching, learning, and talking about race are not allowed in America's schools, then how will our citizens be prepared to interact meaningfully with racially and ethnically diverse citizens elsewhere? They will not be.

Historical Moments of Racial Injustice Will Be Repeated

In lots of ways, many facets of history repeat themselves. It is why history is such an essential subject in our nation's curricula. The suppression of truth-teaching about America's racial past will surely replicate many of our nation's ugliest, deadliest moments. It will not be the fault of today's schoolchildren, who will comprise the next generation of adults. They will not know any better as they engage in the same actions, implement the same policies, and otherwise make the same racial mistakes that prior generations of our nation's citizens made. There is a chance, though, that those inequities and injustices will be even more pronounced and devastating to our democracy next time. Future generations of historians will link various racial disasters that occur throughout the twenty-first century with others like them that occurred in prior periods. Many will likely ask why our country failed to learn from the documented histories that preceded theirs. The suppression of teaching about racial truths will definitely emerge as one of many clear explanations in their analyses.

Americans Will Be Misinformed About What Happened

Today's students will not have full or accurate understandings of what really happened in our nation's history if they are not taught such topics in schools. People of color will experience tremendous gaslighting (or what Frank Harris III and J. Luke Wood have termed "racelighting")[5] as many white Americans attempt to tell them that what happened to their families and communities did not actually happen. Miseducated Americans will have inaccurate and sanitized misunderstandings of how racism and racial inequities became so deeply entrenched into the fabric of our country. One wild example of this is the failed Texas state school board's attempt to replace the word "slavery" with "involuntary relocation" in social studies lessons. Such a revision would have made the horrific enslavement of African peoples in the Americas sound not so bad, like it was not as terrible as Black people keep saying it was. Reparations and other restorative actions will never occur if tomorrow's leaders are denied truths about what actually happened, why it was so awful, and how it has never been adequately addressed.

Racial Tensions and Interracial Conflict Will Intensify

When people do not spend time with people who are different from themselves, they are highly susceptible to developing racist views about those people. Contemporary cohorts of children are already denied rich opportunities for interracial learning and understanding, as residential neighborhoods and K–12 schools in many communities across the country are just about as segregated now as they were prior to the passage of *Brown v. Board of Education*, the landmark US Supreme Court case that was intended to racially integrate educational institutions. Put differently, most students attend K–12 schools with peers who are racially similar to them. A report from the UCLA Civil Rights Project notes the following: "White students, on average, attend a school in which 69 percent of the students are white, while Latino students attend a school in which 55 percent of the students are Latino."[6] The curriculum could be a space in which they are at least introduced to racially diverse others—but not if teaching and learning about those groups' histories, cultures, and full experiences in the US are banned or otherwise suppressed. Those miseducated Americans will then find themselves in workplaces, courtrooms, and other public spaces with persons about whom they know very little. Interracial conflicts are guaranteed to ensue. Moreover, as racial inequities are sustained and exacerbated, people of color are likely to grow even more frustrated with white Americans who do and say racist things.

Americans Will Be Further Conditioned to Ignore Racial Facts

An abundance of trustworthy data sources—state and federal statistics, data from the Centers for Disease Control and the National Institutes of Health, reports from reputable university-based research centers and institutes, and rigorous analyses performed by nonprofit organizations such as the Equal Justice Initiative, Southern Poverty Law Center,

PolicyLink, NAACP Legal Defense Fund, The Joint Center for Political and Economic Studies, The Education Trust, Campaign for College Opportunity, and Economic Policy Institute, to name a few—consistently show that America has a problem with racial inequity. Likewise, thousands of studies published in hundreds of highly respected peer-reviewed academic journals across fields and disciplines document racialized gaps between whites and people of color—with the latter group almost always being on the losing end of those inequities. In other words, the evidence exists, there is lots of it, and the cumulative sum of it is irrefutable. Yet too many Americans have been duped into believing that racism is over and our country does not have serious problems with racial inequities. Too many more will become even further conditioned to ignore facts about race if they are not critically and continuously exposed to them in educational institutions.

Implicit Biases Will Harm and Kill
Even More Americans

Police officers racially profile and kill unarmed Black people, in part, because of implicit racial biases.[7] Women of color die in child birth at higher rates than do white women, in part, because of their doctors' and nurses' implicit racial biases.[8] Black students are suspended and expelled from K–12 schools at disproportionately high rates for engaging in the same or less problematic behaviors than their white peers, in part, because of their teachers' and administrators' implicit racial biases.[9] Applicants of color with so-called ethnic sounding names are routinely discriminated against when applying for jobs, in part, because of employers' implicit racial biases.[10] People of color are severely underrepresented in positions of management and executive-level roles in every industry that comprises our nation's workforce, in part, because of the implicit racial biases that compel white leaders to hire, tap, invest, and promote in their own images.[11] Everyone has implicit biases—people of color and white people alike. If denied opportunities in schools to learn what implicit racial biases are, to examine their own unconscious biases, and to undo problematic prior racial socialization, today's students will become tomorrow's professionals who engage in unintended, harmful, and deadly behaviors. Therefore, truth-teaching must include learning the truth about one's deeply held biases about others.

Even Fewer People of Color Will Enter and Stay in the Teaching Profession

Pew Research Center analyses show that our nation's K–12 teaching workforce slowly diversified between 1988 and 2018.[12] Notwithstanding, nearly 80 percent of today's public school teachers are white.[13] For myriad reasons, entering the education profession is unattractive to an alarmingly high number of citizens across racial and ethnic groups, including women and men who are white. Being forced to lie to children about America's racial past and present is sure to turn away prospective teachers of color whose lived experiences and familial circumstances confirm the realness of the very truths they are not allowed to teach. Being bullied by legislators, fearing the loss of one's job as the occupational penalty for teaching racial topics, and having to pretend that our nation has no problems with race (despite knowing firsthand that it does) will yield two outcomes. First, it will compel many talented professionals of color to say no thanks to even considering becoming teachers. And second, it will be among the factors that drive many excellent teachers of color out of schools and into other professions.

A Nation of Miseducated Adults Will Resent Having Been Lied To

Attacks on truth-teaching will not last forever. This dangerous period of misinformation and disinformation about race in America is not sustainable. Eventually, at some point, professionals who were denied the education they deserved about our nation's racial realities will resent the policymakers who recklessly misled the media, duped families, and made educators lie to them when they were students. Many will come to understand that the racial mistakes they are making at work and the racial conflicts that are ensuing in their communities are largely attributable to the well-funded, politicized campaign that took racial learning and literacy out of schools when they were students. These Americans will not appreciate having to engage in remedial learning. Somehow, they will still love America but hate the lies and incomplete truths they have been taught about it.

Conclusion

I fully acknowledge that my predictions are grim. This is not what I want for America, its citizens, its educational institutions, or its students. In fact, I would like to be wrong. Notwithstanding, I feel confident in these projections. I offer them because I feel a tremendous sense of responsibility as a citizen-scholar to help us take the long view on these dark and dangerous times. My sense is that too many people are misunderstanding the attacks on DEI in schools as a political tide that will soon pass. They seem to think it is largely about a handful of individuals like President Donald Trump or Florida Governor Ron DeSantis or Texas Governor Greg Abbott. As Francesca López, Ashley Burns Nascimiento, and Elisa Serrano so powerfully illustrate in chapter 5 of this book, the recent movement to tear down DEI caught flame quickly and spread like a wildfire all across the country. It seems important to forecast the long-term damage as Americans determine how much effort to place in extinguishing it. Short of a fierce, unified, intergenerational, and interracial campaign to immediately stop the fire from spreading, I am afraid our nation is going to be left with the catastrophic damage described in each of my predictions.

Dispelling "The Big Lie" with Truth-Telling for Justice and Democracy in US Schools

Jaleel R. Howard and Tyrone C. Howard

As "The Big Lie" about race in schools has gained momentum over the past few years, the quest for truth has become increasingly elusive. The avoidance of truth-telling in this highly politicized climate threatens the quality of education for all. Democracy thrives when truth prevails, but it dies when truths are distorted. The current educational moment is situated in a politically charged context that will go down in history as one of the most divisive, confusing, partisan, and perplexing eras in US history.

The prevalence of "fake news" and "alternative facts" has created a reality where one can construct one's own version of reality, thus creating a daunting task for educators who seek truth-telling in their curriculum and instruction. Alternative truths have even more damaging effects when it comes to the education of Black students, who for centuries in this country have been overlooked and underserved in US public schools. The pursuit to identify truths in US history and contemporary events is vital at a time when the persistence of anti-Blackness remains prevalent in schools and society. kihana ross writes about the persistence of anti-Blackness and describes it as a particular form of racism, one steeped in a refusal to acknowledge Black humanity and a disdain and disregard for Black lives.[1]

In an era rife with falsehoods, a collective effort is required by education researchers and practitioners to uphold the truths about various ethnic and racial groups. Access to public education is a fundamental democratic right in the US; therefore, the constant erasure of events, facts, and people is a threat to public education and to people's quest for basic rights. Consider that since 2018 over 535 pieces of anti-LGBTQ+ legislation have been proposed or passed across forty states. Additionally, attacks on race and ethnicity have been persistent over the last four years, with more than thirty states discussing or enacting legislation that bans diversity, equity, and inclusion (DEI) training or content that addresses various aspects of race, racism, inequities, or related concepts. Truth-telling in public education is under attack |

Attacks on truth-telling can also been seen in the recent trend of banning books in school districts across the United States. Eliminating books that document the lives, struggles, and realities of marginalized groups and their fight for humanity should concern us all. Consider that in 2022, the number of banned books surged to troublesome levels. PEN America, which advocates for free creative expression, cited 1,477 instances of books being banned during the first half of the 2022–2023 academic year.[2] Their research has also documented that more than four thousand books have been banned since they started following cases in July 2021.

What is more troubling about the large numbers of books being banned is that 30 percent of the titles are about race or racism, or have main characters of color, while another 26 percent have LGBTQ+ characters or themes. PEN America's research also revealed that Texas led the nation with 438 bans, followed by Florida with 357 and Missouri with 315. Furthermore, at least a dozen other states have at least two hundred book bans, and one can expect that at this pace the numbers will continue to rise. All students should have access to truth when it comes to education. The current moment begs us to ask the questions, Whose truth is being excluded? And why? What steps can be taken to mount an organized and sustained effort for truth, freedom, and equality when it comes to truth-telling?

At this moment, many K–12 teachers feel handcuffed, attacked, and undermined in their ability to teach truth at a time when information is more readily available than it has ever been in our lifetime. Many schools face teacher shortages at a time when they are most needed in schools. One of the primary reasons teachers offer for leaving the profession is that the current political climate is severely restricting what they can and cannot teach.[3] We contend that advocates of truth-telling in public education need to be mindful of five key concepts and strategies that can be used to combat attacks on truth in school: (1) fighting attacks on public education,

(2) increasing political capital, (3) enhancing instructional dexterity, (4) tapping into parental power, and (5) centering students voices. Each of these areas has a tremendous ability to help combat attacks on truth in schools and requires an all-hands-on deck approach to create the types of democratic schools that students deserve.

Fighting Attacks on Public Education

Many of the current indictments of truth-telling education are rooted in calculated and well-funded attacks on public education. While education has historically been considered a public good, it is fair to ask, For whose benefit? There has been a long and sordid history of limiting access to public education to privileged classes. For decades, educational opportunities were denied to Indigenous people, Black people, people of Latin and Asian descent, and those facing economic challenges[4]. The attacks on public education aim to eliminate an institution that has always been regarded as a common good with the potential to be the proverbial equalizer. These attacks are deeply concerning, given that 95 percent of students attend public schools. In many ways, the attacks on critical race theory (CRT), DEI, and "wokeness" are, in essence, attacks on the attempts by public education to become more inclusive in addressing some of the unfortunate and ugly aspects of US history.

Furthermore, one could easily infer that those attacks on "wokeness" are attacks on Blackness. Black people, their histories, and their lived realities are frequently at the center of these truth-telling challenges. Eliminating the depth and breadth of the experiences of Black people in the US prevents us from providing students with a robust understanding of

US history. Moreover, the erasure and dehumanization of Black people in curriculum not only harm Black students but also serve as a catalyst for anti-Blackness amongst non-Black students. Defending public education and seeking truth-telling must have at its core an unrelenting commitment to disrupt anti-Blackness and other forms of bigotry, ensuring that public education is inclusive of the core democratic principles of justice and equality.

Increasing Political Capital

The recent attacks on CRT in many districts and states across the country provide an important playbook for truth-tellers. What is apparent in these attacks on CRT is a well-organized, coordinated, and well-funded effort to craft a narrative that has been essentially untrue from its inception. Consider Moms for Liberty, a conservative political organization that opposes school curricula that mention LGBTQ+ rights, race and ethnicity, CRT, and discrimination. The Southern Poverty Law Center has classified them as an extremist group. However, they have effectively used their platform to mobilize and financially support key political stakeholders who champion their agenda. The ability to bring together stakeholders around various issues that they deem important with a goal of crafting or eliminating legislation is key. Thus, in developing and sustaining political capital in the moment of truth-telling, core legislative issues, such as state funding, curricular requirements, teacher diversity initiatives, elimination of school discipline policies, or the removal of school police, are only a few issues to galvanize around.

Political capital involves the gathering of resources, knowledge, and influence to create just laws, policies, and interventions that can create a political agenda in line with the organizers' set goals. When it comes to political capital and the schooling of Black students, the adoption of Black studies courses that are steeped in truth that includes the contributions of scholars, thinkers, and activists such as bell hooks, Kimberlé Crenshaw, Alice Walker, Toni Morrison, and James Baldwin should be a foundation of this curriculum.

Enhancing Instructional Dexterity

Enhancing instructional dexterity means allowing students to read, reflect, discuss, debate, and participate in a variety of ways to explore content. Truth-telling is centered on allowing students to arrive at their own interpretations, understandings, and conclusions based on information from multiple reliable and fact-based perspectives. Enhancing instructional dexterity is centered on pedagogy that asks students to think critically, reflect, examine, make conceptual connections, problem solve, and utilize other high-engagement cognitive processes, so they come to understand content through active and participatory learning.[5] This approach also provides students the knowledge, skills, and resources to defend their own positions and beliefs in the face of untruths, while methodically disrupting those untruths that they are taught in schools.

So, what does dynamic, stimulating instruction look like? It starts with a teacher explicitly expressing high expectations for students to engage with the content, then involves active learning in which students are positioned to explore, hypothesize, discuss, create, and take risks. Aligned with Freire's concept of problem-posing pedagogy, teachers do not tell students what to think, but instead ask introductory questions to draw students into key concepts, which allows them to develop their own conclusions. However, this can only take place in a learning environment that respects and encourages diverse ways of knowing, thinking, expressing, and interpreting material. Truth-telling in a moment of misinformation and alternate facts requires courageous and bold approaches by teachers to create stimulating learning environments that encourage criticality in a manner that is solution oriented, rooted in conscious raising and intellectual development.[6]

Tapping into Parental Power

One of the most effective strategies conservatives have used to control public education in the United States is mobilizing parental power. Since 2020, there has been a sudden rise of state education laws spearheaded by the right, aimed at restricting what schools can teach and how they teach it, particularly related to topics around race, gender, and sexuality. The success of these new laws is largely due to the participation of predominately conservative (mostly white) parents and caregivers who are determined to have their educational demands met and taught to all students. From Florida to Arizona, and many states in between, conservative groups and politicians have relied on parents to wield their power at school board meetings and other school-sanctioned events to demand a level of power in children's education. This recent demonstration of power by conservatives has allowed for the proliferation of disinformation in many schools across the country and signifies a need for educators on the other end of the political spectrum to tap into the power of likeminded parents.

Research consistently shows that a key factor to student success is parental involvement.[7] Parents are integral to student success primarily because they have the power to impact the decision-making process at schools by participating in school-site parent organizations and voting in large numbers in school board elections. Too often in this recent era of political hostility those on the left often find themselves playing defense; scrambling to combat dehumanizing and discriminatory policies formulated by conservative groups.

Truth-telling efforts must be anchored on new methods to mobilize progressive parents, launch offensive strategies, and mobilize around legislative priorities. Strategies for improving public education that will not be aimed at striking down legislation we disagree with, but instead fighting for legislation that will aid in the creation of safer and more inclusive school environments for all children, must be the goal. To do this, schools need to find innovative strategies to engage parents. Schools have found effective ways to engage wealthy white parents but historically have struggled to form meaningful connections with low-income and minoritized parents.[8]

Centering Students' Voices

Education is a service profession, which means that actions and decisions should be made to better service its clientele, who are students. In other service professions, such as medicine, clients are often asked questions to gauge their needs and preferences to provide optimal care. For example, when someone goes to a doctor's office, a doctor may ask questions like "Tell me why you are here? Where are you feeling pain? How long have you been feeling the pain? What, if anything, have you done at home to ease the pain?" These questions provide practitioners with insights into the best ways to meet their clients' needs. In K–12 schools however, educators rarely take the time to solicit the voices of our clientele, which inevitably hinders our ability to deliver high-quality service. In postsecondary settings, students are afforded the opportunity to evaluate their educators every semester. Therefore, we understand the significance of student perspectives in higher education. So, why do we not center student voices in K–12 schools? Centering student voices will allow us to better design our school practices and policy around student needs.

Furthermore, centering the voices of students of color, who are often rendered voiceless in educational discourse, is crucial for disrupting the rampant harm inflicted upon students of color in K–12 schools. Listening to what students want to learn in schools is vital in a truth-telling moment. What must be rejected is the idea that students cannot articulate or express the type of truth-telling they want in schools. The levels of intelligence, critical thinking, and creativity of today's student body is perhaps unmatched by any generation of young people. Listening is learning, and truth-telling thrives when those who are being served have their voices valued.

Numerous scholars have argued that in order to improve schools, we must engage students in meaningful discourse.[9] Schools benefit from interrogating the perspectives of their students because it reveals what is working to enhance student success and what is subverting the potential of their student body. Centering student voices does not mean merely providing a space for students to share their grievances, but actively working toward transforming learning environments based on the information gathered from students. The truth is that schools in the United States still have not found ways to effectively educate students of nondominant backgrounds and consistently rely on researchers and policy makers to solve this quandary. The need for racial literacy is essential in a truth-telling era. The lack of success in improve educational outcomes should push all educators to engage the most important stakeholders in the educational equation, which is students.

Conclusion

What cannot be ignored in the current era of attacks on truth is the role that race, and racism, plays in such efforts. The ongoing attacks on public education are a painful reminder of the power of whiteness, privilege that allows for the erasure and silencing of important aspects of the US narrative where non-white populations are concerned. Truth-telling emerges when courageous truth-tellers dare to speak truth to power. In this moment, there is a need for a diverse coalition of voices to speak loudly, boldly, and fiercely. For too long, it has largely been people of color who have been on the frontlines fighting for truth and inclusion. We explicitly call for white parents, practitioners, and researchers who do not agree with recent conservative attacks on education to step up and be coconspirators in the pursuit of truth in public education. True allies are needed. This is not the time to be satisfied with reading the latest antiracism self-help book or eating at a local Black-owned restaurant. What is needed are allies to use their privilege and actively participate in school board meetings, voting booths, and PTA meetings, standing alongside parents of color in their advocacy for truth. Democracy thrives when we listen to a collective majority rather than a powerful few. Countering The Big Lie about race in schools requires organized collaboration and advocacy from a diverse group of stakeholders who are willing to defend public education.

NOTES

FOREWORD

1. H. Richard Milner, *The Race Card: Leading the Fight for Truth in America's Schools* (Thousand Oaks, CA: Corwin, 2023).
2. Derrick Bell, "Racial Realism," *Connecticut Law Review* 24, no. 2 (1992), 363–80.

CHAPTER I

1. Sarah Schwartz and Evie Blad, "Map: Where Critical Race Theory Is Under Attack," *Education Week*, June 11, 2021, https://www.edweek.org/policy-politics/map-where-critical-race-theory-is-under-attack/2021/06.
2. Jake Silverstein, "Why We Published the 1619 Project," *New York Times Magazine*, December 20, 2019, https://www.nytimes.com/interactive/2019/12/20/magazine/1619-intro.html.
3. Silverstein, "Why We Published."
4. Jeff Barrus, "Pulitzer Center Named Education Partner for The New York Times Magazine's 'The 1619 Project,'" Pulitzer Center, August 14, 2019, https://pulitzercenter.org/blog/pulitzer-center-named-education-partner-new-york-times-magazines-1619-project.
5. Jon Sawyer, Emily Rauh Pulitzer, and Lucille Crelli, "2019 Pulitzer Center Annual Report," Pulitzer Center, December 31, 2019, https://pulitzercenter.org/blog/2019-pulitzer-center-annual-report.

6. Leslie M. Harris, "I Helped Fact-Check the 1619 Project. The Times Ignored Me," March 6, 2020, Politico, https://www .politico.com/news/magazine/2020/03/06/1619-project-new -york-times-mistake-122248.

7. Harris, "I Helped Fact-Check."

8. Jake Silverstein, "We Respond to the Historians Who Critiqued the 1619 Project," *New York Times Magazine*, December 20, 2019, https://www.nytimes.com/2019/12/20/magazine/we-respond -to-the-historians-who-critiqued-the-1619-project.html.

9. J. Brian Charles, "The New York Times 1619 Project Is Re-shaping the Conversation on Slavery. Conservatives Hate It," *Vox*, August 19, 2019, https://www.vox.com/identities/2019/8 /19/20812238/1619-project-slavery-conservatives.

10. Congress.gov, "S.4292 - 116th Congress (2019–2020): Saving American History Act of 2020," July 23, 2020, https://www .congress.gov/bill/116th-congress/senate-bill/4292.

11. Black Lives Matter, "About," https://blacklivesmatter.com /about/.

12. Gustavo Solis, "What We Know (and Don't Know) so Far About the Effort to Dismantle the Minneapolis Police De-partment," MinnPost, July 2020, https://www.minnpost.com /metro/2020/07/what-we-know-and-dont-know-so-far-about -the-effort-to-dismantle-the-minneapolis-police-department/.

13. Eric Fitzhugh et al., "It's Time for a New Approach to Racial Equity," McKinsey & Company, 2020, https://www.mckinsey .com/bem/our-insights/its-time-for-a-new-approach-to -racial-equity.

14. Jay Hartzell, "A More Diverse and Welcoming Campus," Office of the President, The University of Texas at Austin, July 13, 2020, https://president.utexas.edu/messages-speeches -2020/a-more-diverse-and-welcoming-campus.

15. Joel Shannon, "Report Counts How Many Confederate Stat-ues Have Been Removed Since George Floyd's Death. It's a Lot," *USA Today*, August 12, 2020, https://www.usatoday.com /story/news/nation/2020/08/12/george-floyd-confederate -monuments-splc/3356819001/.

16. Benjamin Wallace-Wells, "How a Conservative Activist In-vented the Conflict over Critical Race Theory," *New Yorker*,

June 18, 2021, https://www.newyorker.com/news/annals-of -inquiry/how-a-conservative-activist-invented-the-conflict -over-critical-race-theory.

17. Christopher F. Rufo, "Separate but Equal," July 29, 2020, https://christopherrufo.com/separate-but-equal/.

18. Wallace-Wells, "Conservative Activist."

19. San Dorman, "Chris Rufo Calls on Trump to End Critical Race Theory 'Cult Indoctrination' in Federal Government," Fox News, September 1, 2020, https://www.foxnews.com /politics/chris-rufo-race-theory-cult-federal-government.

20. Matthew S. Schwartz, "Trump Tells Agencies to End Trainings on 'White Privilege' and 'Critical Race Theory,'" NPR, September 5, 2020, https://www.npr.org/2020/09/05/910053496 /trump-tells-agencies-to-end-trainings-on-white-privilege-and -critical-race-theor.

21. The White House, "Memorandum for the Heads of Executive Departments and Agencies," September 2020, https://www .whitehouse.gov/wp-content/uploads/2020/09/M-20-34.pdf.

22. The White House, "Executive Order on Combating Race and Sex Stereotyping," Trump White House Archives," https:// trumpwhitehouse.archives.gov/presidential-actions/executive -order-combating-race-sex-stereotyping/.

23. The White House, "Executive Order."

24. Idaho Legislature, "HB 377," 2021, https://legislature.idaho .gov/wp-content/uploads/sessioninfo/2021/legislation /H0377.pdf.

25. Montana Department of Justice, "AGO-V58-O1–5.27.21- FINAL," 2021, https://dojmt.gov/wp-content/uploads/AGO -V58-O1-5.27.21-FINAL.pdf.

26. Florida Senate, "Bill Text: ER—2022–7," 2022, https://www .flsenate.gov/Session/Bill/2022/7/BillText/er/pdf.

27. Florida Senate, "Bill Text: ER—2022–7."

28. The Heritage Foundation, "States Use Heritage's Model Legislation to Reject Critical Race Theory in Classrooms," https:// www.heritage.org/education/impact/states-use-heritages -model-legislation-reject-critical-race-theory-classrooms.

29. Adam Barnes, "Texas and Florida Take Steps to Limit Professor Tenure at State Schools," The Hill, April 21, 2022,

https://thehill.com/changing-america/enrichment/education /3274661-texas-and-florida-take-steps-to-limit-professor -tenure-at-state-schools/.

30. PEN America and American Association of Colleges and Universities (AACU), "Statement by the American Association of Colleges and Universities (AAC&U) and PEN America Regarding Recent Legislative Restrictions on Teaching and Learning," 2022, https://pen.org/wp-content/uploads/2022 /06/Statement-by-AACU-and-PEN-2.pdf.

31. Indiana General Assembly, "HB1040—Introduced," 2022, https://legiscan.com/IN/text/HB1040/id/2462805/Indiana -2022-HB1040-Introduced.pdf.

32. Hannah Natanson, "A White Teacher Taught White Students About White privilege. It Cost Him His Job," *Washington Post*, December 6, 2021, https://www.washingtonpost.com /education/2021/12/06/tennessee-teacher-fired-critical-race -theory/.

33. Hannah Natanson and Moriah Balingit, "Caught in the Culture Wars, Teachers Are Being Forced from Their Jobs," *Washington Post*, June 16, 2022, https://www.washingtonpost .com/education/2022/06/16/teacher-resignations-firings -culture-wars/.

34. Brian Lopez, "How a Black High School Principal Was Swept into a 'Critical Race Theory' Maelstrom in a Mostly White Texas Suburb," *Texas Tribune*, September 18, 2021, https:// www.texastribune.org/2021/09/18/colleyville-principal -critical-race-theory/.

35. Ibram X. Kendi, *How to Be an Antiracist* (London: One World, 2023).

CHAPTER 2

1. Morgan Chalfant, "Trump: 'The only way we're going to lose this election is if the election is rigged,'" The Hill, August 17, 2020, https://thehill.com/homenews/administration/512424 -trump-the-only-way-we-are-going-to-lose-this-election-is-if -the/.

2. United States House of Representatives, "Final Report of the Select Committee to Investigate the January 6th Attack on

the United States Capitol," December 22, 2022, https://www
.govinfo.gov/content/pkg/GPO-J6-REPORT/pdf/GPO-J6
-REPORT.pdf.

3. James C. Bridgeforth, "'This Isn't Who We Are': A Critical
   Discourse Analysis of School and District Leaders' Responses
   to Racial Violence in Schools," *Journal of School Leadership* 31,
   no. 1–2 (2021): 85–106.

4. National Center for Education Statistics, "Characteristics
   of Public School Teachers. Condition of Education," U.S.
   Department of Education, Institute of Education Sciences,
   May 2023, https://nces.ed.gov/programs/coe/indicator/clr.

5. National Center for Education Statistics, "Full-Time Faculty
   in Degree-Granting Postsecondary Institutions, by Race/
   Ethnicity, Sex, and Academic Rank: Fall 2019, Fall 2020, and
   Fall 2021," Digest of Education Statistics, US Department
   of Education, Institute of Education Sciences, January 2023,
   https://nces.ed.gov/programs/digest/d22/tables/dt22_315.20
   .asp.

6. Melissa Fuesting, "The Higher Ed Admissions Workforce:
   Pay, Diversity, Equity, and Years in Position," College and
   University Professional Association for Human Resources,
   April 2023, https://www.cupahr.org/surveys/research-briefs
   /the-higher-ed-admissions-workforce-april-2023.

7. Richard Lowery v. Texas A&M University System, 4:22-cv-
   3091 TX (2022), https://fingfx.thomsonreuters.com/gfx
   /legaldocs/lgpdwdxdrvo/EMPLOYMENT_TEXASAM
   _DIVERSITY_complaint.pdf.

8. Texas A&M University Human Resources, "Fall 2022
   Workforce Profile," https://employees.tamu.edu/talent
   -management/_media/workforce/2022%20Part%2002.pdf.

9. S. R. Harper and S. Hurtado, "Nine Themes in Campus
   Racial Climates and Implications for Institutional Trans-
   formation," in "Responding to the Realities of Race on
   Campus," ed. S. R. Harper and L. D. Patton, special issue,
   New Directions for Student Services 2007, no. 120 (Winter
   2007): 7–24.

10. Summer Lin and Noah Goldberg, "Black Students at Up-
    land Elementary School Reportedly Bullied with Racist

Drawings," *Los Angeles Times*, February 21, 2023, https://www
.latimes.com/california/story/2023-02-21/racist-incidents
-upland-pepper-tree-elementary-school.

11. "Black Students Receive Racist Drawings at California
Elementary School," CNN, February 23, 2023, https://www
.cnn.com/videos/us/2023/02/23/racist-drawings-california
-elementary-school-black-students-cnntm-lah-pkg-vpx.cnn.

12. University of Virginia, "President Sullivan Condemns
Demonstration Violence," https://news.virginia.edu/content
/president-sullivan-condemns-demonstration-violence?utm
_source=UTwitter&utm_medium=social&utm_campaign
=news#sullivan_statement.

13. Shaun R. Harper and Charles H.F. Davis III, "What UVA
Did Wrong When White Supremacists Came to Campus,"
Los Angeles Times, August 12, 2017, https://www.latimes.com
/opinion/op-ed/la-oe-harper-davis-uva-white-supremacists
-20170812-story.html.

14. Mitchell J. Chang, "The Impact of an Undergraduate Diversity
Course Requirement on Students' Racial Views and Attitudes,"
Journal of General Education 51, no. 1 (2002): 21–42.

15. Anjali Adukia et al., "What We Teach About Race and Gender: Representation in Images and Text of Children's Books,"
Quarterly Journal of Economics, 138, no. 4 (November 2023):
2225–85, https://doi.org/10.1093/qje/qjad028.

16. Lori D. Patton, *Culture Centers in Higher Education* (Sterling,
VA: Stylus, 2010).

17. National Association of Diversity Officers in Higher Education, "State of the CDO Survey Report," August 2023,
https://nadohe.memberclicks.net/assets/2023/State-of-the
-CDO.pdf.

18. Jack Stripling, "DeSantis Signs Bill to Defund DEI Programs
at Florida's Public Colleges," *Washington Post*, May 15, 2023,
https://www.washingtonpost.com/education/2023/05/15
/desantis-defunds-dei-programs-florida-colleges.

19. Marcela Rodrigues, "Gov. Abbott Signs DEI Bill into Law,
Dismantling Diversity Offices at Colleges," *Dallas Morning
News*, June 14, 2023, https://www.dallasnews.com/news

/education/2023/06/14/gov-abbott-signs-dei-bill-into-law
-dismantling-diversity-offices-at-colleges.

20. Harm Venhuizen, "Universities of Wisconsin Unveil Plan to
Recover $32 Million Cut by Republicans in Diversity Fight,"
Associated Press, November 6, 2023, https://apnews.com
/article/universities-wisconsin-legislature-diversity-funding
-plan-255fd51e5e5caaa1701c337660db0ec2.

21. Board of Regents, University of Wisconsin System, "About
the Universities of Wisconsin," March 2024, https://www
.wisconsin.edu/about.

22. Derrick A. Bell, "Who's Afraid of Critical Race Theory?" *University of Illinois Law Review*, 1995, no. 4: 893–910.

CHAPTER 3

1. Derrick Bell, *Faces at the Bottom of the Well: The Permanence of
Racism* (New York: Basic Books, 2018), 246–47.

2. Shaun Harper, "Why Politicized Attacks on DEI in Schools
are Occurring, and How They're Bad for America," *Forbes*,
June 9, 2023, https://www.forbes.com/sites/shaunharper
/2023/06/09/why-politicized-attacks-on-dei-in-schools
-are-occurring-and-how-theyre-bad-for-america/?sh
=7972d68414c7; Francesca López and Christine E. Sleeter,
Critical Race Theory and Its Critics (New York: Teachers College
Press, 2023).

3. Sarah Schwartz, "Map: Where Critical Race Theory is Under
Attack," *Education Week*, June 13, 2023, https://www.edweek
.org/policy-politics/map-where-critical-race-theory-is-under
-attack/2021/06.

4. Jonathan Friedman and Nadine Farid Johnson, "Banned
in the USA: The Growing Movement to Censor Books in
Schools," PEN America, September 19, 2022, https://pen.org
/report/banned-usa-growing-movement-to-censor-books-in
-schools/; Kasey Meehan and Jonathan Friedman, "Banned
in the USA: State Laws Supercharge Book Suppression in
Schools," PEN America, April 20, 2023, https://pen.org
/report/banned-in-the-usa-state-laws-supercharge-book
-suppression-in-schools/; Eesha Pendharkar, "Who's Behind

the Escalating Push to Ban Books? A New Report Has Answers," *Education Week*, September 28, 2022, https://www .edweek.org/leadership/whos-behind-the-escalating-push -to-ban-books-a-new-report-has-answers/2022/09; Eesha Pendharkar, "As Book Bans Escalate, Here's What You Need to Know," *Education Week*, September 30, 2022, https://www .edweek.org/teaching-learning/as-book-bans-escalate-heres -what-you-need-to-know/2022/09.

5. Timothy Bella, "A Black Principal Was Accused of Embrac-ing Critical Race Theory in the Classroom. He's Now Out of a Job," *Washington Post*, November 10, 2021, https://www .washingtonpost.com/education/2021/11/10/texas-principal -critical-race-theory-whitfield/; Elizabeth Green, "He Taught a Ta-Nehisi Coates Essay. Then He Was Fired," *The Atlantic*, August 17, 2021, https://www.theatlantic.com/politics /archive/2021/08/matt-hawn-tennessee-teacher-fired-white -privilege/619770/; Anneta Konstantinides, "A Teacher Who Spoke Out After Her Students Were Banned from Singing 'Rainbowland' by Dolly Parton and Miley Cyrus Has Been Fired," *Yahoo! News*, July 13, 2023, https://news.yahoo.com /teacher-spoke-her-students-were-174050892.html; Claudette Riley, "Southwest Missouri High School Teacher Accused of Using Critical Race Theory Loses Job," *Springfield News-Leader*, April 7, 2022, https://www.news-leader.com/story/news /education/2022/04/07/greenfield-missouri-teacher-kim -morrison-accused-teaching-critical-race-theory-crt-loses -job/7264924001/; Katie Shepherd, "Texas Parents Accused a Black Principal of Promoting Critical Race Theory. The Dis-trict Has Now Suspended Him," *Washington Post*, September 1, 2021, https://www.washingtonpost.com/nation/2021/09/01 /texas-principal-critical-race-theory/.

6. Jonathan Friedman, "Goodbye Red Scare, Hello Ed Scare," *Inside Higher Education*, February 23, 2022, https://www .insidehighered.com/views/2022/02/24/higher-ed-must-act -against-educational-gag-orders-opinion; Linda Stamato, "Commentary: The 'Ed Scare' Takes Hold in America," *Morris-town Green*, March 2, 2022, https://morristowngreen.com/2022 /03/02/commentary-the-ed-scare-takes-hold-in-america/.

7. Charles M. Blow, "L.G.B.T.Q. Americans Could Become a 'New Class of Political Refugees,'" *New York Times*, June 14, 2023, https://www.nytimes.com/2023/06/14/opinion /transgender-florida.html.

8. Erin Blakemore, "The History of Book Bans—and Their Changing Targets—in the U.S.," *National Geographic*, April 24, 2023, https://www.nationalgeographic.com/culture/article /history-of-book-bans-in-the-united-states.

9. "Bannings and Burnings in History," Freedom to Read. https://www.freedomtoread.ca/resources/bannings-and -burnings-in-history/.

10. Katherine Schulten, "Banned Books, Censored Topics: Teaching About the Battle over What Students Should Learn," *New York Times*, September 22, 2022, https://www.nytimes.com /2022/09/22/learning/lesson-plans/banned-books-censored -topics-teaching-about-the-battle-over-what-students-should -learn.html.

11. Trisha Tucker, "Dangerous Reading: How Socially Constructed Narratives of Childhood Shape Perspectives on Book Banning," *Public Library Quarterly*, 2023. https://doi.org /10.1080/01616846.2023.2232289.

12. "Voters Oppose Book Bans in Libraries," American Library Association, March 1–6, 2022, https://www.ala.org/advocacy /voters-oppose-book-bans-libraries.

13. Hannah Natanson, "Objection to Sexual, LGBTQ Content Propels Spike in Book Challenges: An Analysis of Book Challenges from Across the Nation Shows the Majority Were Filed by Just 11 People," *Washington Post*, May 23, 2023, updated June 9, 2023, https://www.washingtonpost.com/education /2023/05/23/lgbtq-book-ban-challengers/.

14. Bettina L. Love, "No, Public Education Isn't Too Woke. It's Barely Even Awake," *Education Week*, July 14, 2023, https:// www.edweek.org/leadership/opinion-no-public-education -isnt-too-woke-its-barely-even-awake/2023/07.

15. Brittany Aronson and Judson Laughter, "The Theory and Practice of Culturally Relevant Education: A Synthesis of Research Across Content Areas," *Review of Educational Research*, 86, no. 1 (2016): 163–206; Samantha Putterman,

"Politifact FL: DeSantis Says He Removed CRT from K-12 Schools. Districts Say It Wasn't Taught," WMFE 90.7, August 14, 2023, https://www.wmfe.org/politics/2023-08-14/desantis-critical-race-theory-florida-schools; López and Sleeter, *Critical Race Theory*.

16. James Tager and Clarisse Rosaz Shariyf, "Reading Between the Lines: Race, Equity, and Book Publishing," PEN America, October 17, 2022, https://pen.org/report/race-equity-and-book-publishing/.

17. Lori D. Patton, Shaun R. Harper, and Jessica Harris, "Using Critical Race Theory to (Re)Interpret Widely Studied Topics Related to Students in U.S. Higher Education," in *Critical Approaches to the Study of Higher Education: A Practical Introduction*, ed. Ana M. Martínez-Alemán, Brian Pusser, and Estela Mara Bensimon (Baltimore, MD: Johns Hopkins University Press, 2015, 193–219); Janine de Novais and George Spencer, "Learning Race to Unlearn Racism: The Effects of Ethnic Studies Course-Taking," *The Journal of Higher Education* 90, no. 6 (2019), 860–83, https://doi.org/10.1080/00221546.2018.1545498.

18. Shilpi Sinha and Shaireen Rasheed, "Journeying Toward Transformative Teaching in the Age of Alternative Facts and Re-Ascendent Ethnic and Racial Prejudice," *Teachers College Record* 22 (April 2020).

19. López and Sleeter, *Critical Race Theory*.

20. Wesley Lowery, *American Whitelash: A Changing Nation and the Cost of Progress* (New York: Mariner Books, 2023).

21. López and Sleeter, *Critical Race Theory*, 42–43.

22. "What Is PEN America?" PEN America. https://pen.org/about-us/.

23. "PEN America v. Escambia County School District," PEN America, https://pen.org/pen-america-v-escambia-county/.

24. "We're Fighting Censorship: Legal Action," Penguin Random House, https://www.penguinrandomhouse.com/articles/what-were-doing-legal-action/.

25. "Advocating for Change—Racial and Social Justice," National Education Association, https://www.nea.org/advocating-for-change/racial-social-justice.

26. López and Sleeter, *Critical Race Theory*, 94–96.

27. López and Sleeter, 103.

28. John Pascarella and Erica Silva, "How Can K-12 Leaders Advance Racial Equity in the Face of Book Bans and Censorship Measures?" USC Race and Equity Center, Spring 2023, https://race.usc.edu/wp-content/uploads/2023/05/Pascarella -Silva-2023-K-12-Equity-Leadership-Brief.pdf.

29. Daniel Liou and Kelly Deits Cutler, "A Framework for Resisting Book Bans," Association for Supervision and Curriculum Development, https://www.ascd.org/el/articles/a-framework -for-resisting-book-bans.

30. Bell, *Bottom of the Well*, 246–47.

CHAPTER 4

1. Eesha Pendharkar, "State Laws Are Behind Many Book Bans, Even Indirectly, Report Finds," *Education Week*, May 19, 2023, https://www.edweek.org/teaching-learning/state-laws-are -behind-many-book-bans-even-indirectly-report-finds/2023 /05; Taifha Alexander et al., "CRT Forward: Tracking the Attack on Critical Race Theory," 2023, https://crtforward .law.ucla.edu/wp-content/uploads/2023/04/UCLA-Law_CRT -Report_Final.pdf.

2. Tim Walker, "Teaching in an Era of Polarization," *NEA Today*, July 14, 2021. https://www.nea.org/advocating-for-change /new-from-nea/teaching-era-polarization.

3. Myles Horton, *We Make the Road by Walking: Conversations on Education and Social Change* (Philadelphia: Temple University Press, 1990).

4. Yolanda Sealey-Ruiz, "Archeology of Self," https://www .yolandasealeyruiz.com/archaeology-of-self.

5. Sonja Cherry-Paul, "Culturally Relevant Pedagogy: Implications for Reading and Writing Workshop" (presentation at the Cotsen Foundation for the Art of Teaching Annual Conference 2022, Long Beach, CA, June 16, 2022); Gloria Ladson-Billings, "But That's Just Good Teaching! The Case for Culturally Relevant Pedagogy," *Theory into Practice* 34, no. 3 (1995): 159–65, doi.org/10.1080/00405849509543675.

6. Gloria Ladson-Billings, "Toward a Theory of Culturally Relevant Pedagogy," *American Educational Research Journal*

32, no. 3 (1995): 465–91, doi.org/10.2307/1163320; Brandon Girod, "Florida Approves Prager U Curriculum: Why Critics Are Sounding the Alarm on Right-wing Bias,"*USA Today*, August 1, 2023, https://www.usatoday.com/story/news/nation/2023/08/01/prageru-curriculum-florida-schools/70505340007/; Jack Dura, "Buckle Up: New Laws from Seat Belts to Library Books Take Effect in North Dakota," Associated Press, July 29, 2023, https://apnews.com/article/north-dakota-legislature-laws-929c5ce7eda9e6e 8c6daafd 372852bc5; Tony Kurzweil, "School District Rejects California's New Social Studies Book, Drawing Ire of Gov. Newsom," KTLA, July 19, 2023, https://ktla.com/news/local-news/school-district-rejects-californias-new-social-studies-book-drawing-ire-of-gov-newsom/.

7. Niral Shah and Justin A. Coles, "Preparing Teachers to Notice Race in Classrooms: Contextualizing the Competencies of Preservice Teachers with Antiracist Inclinations," *Journal of Teacher Education* 71, no. 5 (2020): 584–99, doi.org/10.1177/0022487119900204.

8. Diana Lambert, "Conservatives Are Waging a War for Control over California School Boards," *EdSource*, October 13, 2022, https://edsource.org/2022/conservatives-are-waging-a-war-for-control-over-california-school-boards/679713.

CHAPTER 5

1. Mica Pollock et al., "The Conflict Campaign: Exploring Local Experiences of the Campaign to Ban 'Critical Race Theory' in Public K–12 Education in the US, 2020–2021," https://idea.gseis.ucla.edu/publications/the-conflict-campaign/.

2. Ashley Jochim et al., "Navigating Political Tensions over Schooling: Findings from the Fall 2022 American School District Panel Survey," 2023, https://crpe.org/asdp-2023-politics-brief/.

3. Tess Bissell, "Teaching in the Upside Down: What Anti-Critical Race Theory Laws Tell Us About the First Amendment," *Stanford Law Review* 75 (2023): 205.

4. A. Ma, C. Lauer, and A. G. Licón, "As Conservatives Target Schools, LGBTQ+ Kids and Students of Color Feel Less

Safe," Associated Press, June 7, 2023, https://apnews.com /article/lgbtq-race-ban-schools-4c4df1728f5265eee36842680 35570c2.

5. Jochim et al., "Navigating Political Tensions."

6. J. Rogers, and J. Kahne, with M. Ishimoto et al., *Educating for a Diverse Democracy: The Chilling Role of Political Conflict in Blue, Purple, and Red Communities* (Los Angeles: UCLA Institute for Democracy, Education, and Access, 2022), 24.

7. U. M. Jayakumar and R. Kohli, "Silenced and Pushed Out: The Harms of CRT-Bans on K-12 Teachers" *Thresholds in Education* 46, no. 1 (Winter 2023): 96–113; Jochim et al., "Navigating Political Tensions."

8. M. Levy, "Burnout, Low Pay and Politics are Driving away Teachers. Turnover Is Soaring for Educators of Color," Associated Press, August 2, 2023, https://apnews.com/article/teacher -retirement-quit-job-b0c39ec0d4320e12f2767a342e503f85.

9. "Going Beyond the Headlines: New National Research Reveals Strong Agreement Among K-12 Parents, Teachers & Principals," Learning Heroes, December 2021, https://media .carnegie.org/filer_public/4c/80/4c8060da-a395-4771-a307 -8eae283865ac/parents-2021.pdf.

10. Man-pui Sally Chan and Dolores Albarracín, "A Meta-Analysis of Correction Effects in Science-Relevant Misinformation," *Nature Human Behaviour* 7 (2023): 1–12.

11. Francesca López and Christine E. Sleeter, *Critical Race Theory and Its Critics: Implications for Research and Teaching* (New York, NY: Teachers College Press, 2023).

12. Pavlos Vasilopoulos et al., "Fear, Anger, and Voting for the Far Right: Evidence from the November 13, 2015 Paris Terror Attacks," *Political Psychology* 40, no. 4 (2019): 679–704.

13. Lauren McDonald, "Think Tanks and the Media: How the Conservative Movement Gained Entry into the Education Policy Arena," *Educational Policy* 28, no. 6 (2014): 845–880.

14. Marie-Laure Djelic, "Spreading Ideas to Change the World: Inventing and Institutionalizing the Neoliberal Think Tank," in *Political Affair: Bridging Markets and Politics*, ed. Christina Garsten and Adrienne Sörbom (Cheltenham, UK: Edward Elgar, 2014), 3.

15. David C. Berliner and Gene V. Glass, ed, *50 Myths and Lies that Threaten America's Public Schools: The Real Crisis in Education* (New York: Teachers College Press, 2014); Diane Ravitch, *Slaying Goliath: The Passionate Resistance to Privatization and the Fight to Save America's Public Schools* (New York: Vintage Books, 2020).

16. Francesca López et al., *Understanding the Attacks on Critical Race Theory* (Boulder, CO: National Education Policy Center, 2021), https://nepc.colorado.edu/sites/default/files/publications/PM%20Lopez%20CRT_0.pdf.

17. E. J. Fagan, *Information Wars: Party Elites, Think Tanks and Polarization in Congress* (New York: Oxford University Press, 2024); McDonald, "Think Tanks and the Media."

18. Fagan, *Information Wars*.

19. J. Butcher and M. Gonzalez, "Critical Race Theory, the New Intolerance, and Its Grip on America" Backgrounder no. 3567, The Heritage Foundation, December 7, 2020, http://report.heritage.org/bg3567.

20. "PEN America Index of Educational Gag Orders," https://docs.google.com/spreadsheets/d/1Tj5WQVBmB6SQg-zP_M8uZsQQGH09TxmBY73v23zpyr0/edit#gid=1505554870.

21. McDonald, "Think Tanks and the Media," 852–54.

22. Pollock et al., "The Conflict Campaign."

23. Pollock et al., vii.

24. Pollock et al.

25. "Chris Rufo Calls on Trump to End Critical Race Theory 'Cult Indoctrination' in Federal Government," Fox News, September 2, 2020, https://www.foxnews.com/politics/chris-rufo-race-theory-cult-federal-government.

26. B. Wallace-Wells, "How a Conservative Activist Invented the Conflict over Critical Race Theory," *The New Yorker*, June 18, 2021, www.newyorker.com/news/annals-of-inquiry/how-a-conservative-activist-invented-the-conflict-over-critical-race-theory.

27. Mary Ellen Flannery, "Voters and Parents Trust Teachers, New Poll Finds, *NEA News*, September 9, 2022, https://www.nea.org/nea-today/all-news-articles/voters-and-parents-trust-teachers-new-poll-finds.

28. Flannery, "Voters and Parents Trust Teachers."
29. FrameWorks Institute, "Making the Case for Equitable and Just Public Education," https://www.frameworksinstitute .org/wp-content/uploads/2020/06/sharedstory-messaging strategies.pdf, 2.
30. Jochim et al., "Navigating Political Tensions"; López and Sleeter, *Critical Race Theory.*
31. Chan and Albarracín, "A Meta-Analysis."
32. D. López Gonzales and R. Wiener, "United We Learn: Honoring America's Racial and Ethnic Diversity in Education," The Aspen Institute, 2021, https://www.aspeninstitute.org /publications/united-we-learn/
33. Ross Wiener and Francesca López, "Ignoring Racism in School Actually Increases Racism, *Education Week*, March 29, 2022, https://www.edweek.org/teaching-learning/opinion -ignoring-racism-in-schools-actually-increases-prejudice /2022/03.
34. Julie Sweetland, Marisa Gerstein Pineau, and Moira O'Neill, "Advancing Anti-Racist Education: How School Leaders Can Navigate the Moral Panic about 'Critical Race Theory,'" FrameWorks, December 2022, https://www .frameworksinstitute.org/wp-content/uploads/2023/01 /advancing-antiracist-education_Dec2022.pdf.
35. Sweetland, Pineau, and O'Neill, "Advancing Anti-Racist Education."
36. Ian Haney Lopez, *Merge Left: Fusing Race and Class, Winning Elections, and Saving America.* New York: New Press, 2019).
37. Sweetland, Pineau, and O'Neill, "Advancing Anti-Racist Education."
38. Sweetland, Pineau, and O'Neill, 10.
39. FrameWorks Institute, "Making the Case."
40. Sweetland, Pineau, and O'Neill, "Advancing Anti-Racist Education."
41. Matt Gertz, "Fox's Anti-'Critical Race Theory' Parents Are Also GOP Activists," Media Matters, June 17, 2021. www .mediamatters.org/fox-news/foxs-anti-critical-race-theory -parents-are-also-gop-activists.
42. Jochim et al., "Navigating Political Tensions," 5.

CHAPTER 6

1. Executive Order no. 13950. https://www.dol.gov/agencies/ofccp/executive-order-13950.

2. Sarah Schwartz, "Map: Where Critical Race Theory Is Under Attack," *Education Week*, June 11, 2021, https://www.edweek.org/policy-politics/map-where-critical-race-theory-is-under-attack/2021/06.

3. Staff, "Governor Ron DeSantis Signs Legislation to Protect Floridians from Discrimination and Woke Indoctrination," April 22, 2022, https://www.flgov.com/2022/04/22/governor-ron-desantis-signs-legislation-to-protect-floridians-from-discrimination-and-woke-indoctrination/.

4. Eesha Pendharker, "Florida's Ban on AP African American Studies, Explained." *Education Week*, January 25, 2023, https://www.edweek.org/teaching-learning/floridas-ban-on-ap-african-american-studies-explained/2023/01.

5. Sam Cabral, "Florida's New Black History Curriculum 'Sanitised', Say Critics," BBC News, July 20, 2023, https://www.bbc.com/news/world-us-canada-66261072; Florida Department of Education, "Florida's State Academic Standards: Social Studies," https://www.fldoe.org/academics/standards/subject-areas/social-studies/african-amer-hist.stml.

6. E. J. R. David, Tiera M. Schroeder, and Jessica Anne Fernandez, "Internalized Racism: A Systematic Review of the Psychological Literature on Racism's Most Insidious Consequence," *Journal of Social Issues* 75, no. 4 (2019): 1057–86; Katherine Kirkinis et al., "Racism, Racial Discrimination, and Trauma: A Systematic Review of the Social Science Literature," *Ethnicity & Health* 26, no. 3 (2021): 392–412.

7. Brown v. Board of Education, 347 U.S. 483 (1954); Ludy T. Benjamin Jr. and Ellen M. Crouse, "The American Psychological Association's Response to Brown v. Board of Education: The Case of Kenneth B. Clark," *American Psychologist* 57, no. 1 (2002): 38–50.

8. Robert Carter, "Racism and Psychological and Emotional Injury: Recognizing and Assessing Race-Based Traumatic Stress," *The Counseling Psychologist* 35, no. 1 (2007): 13–105; Lillian Comas-Díaz, Gordon Nagayama Hall, and Helen A.

Neville, "Racial Trauma: Theory, Research, and Healing: Introduction to the Special Issue," *American Psychologist* 74, no. 1 (2019): 1–5.

9. Farzana T. Saleem, Riana E. Anderson, and Monnica Williams, "Addressing the "Myth" of Racial Trauma: Developmental and Ecological Considerations for Youth of Color," *Clinical Child and Family Psychology Review* 23, (2020): 1–14.

10. Leah Cave et al., "Racial Discrimination and Child and Adolescent Health in Longitudinal Studies: A Systematic Review," *Social Science & Medicine,* 250 (2020): 112864.

11. Keith Churchwell et al., "Call to Action: Structural Racism as a Fundamental Driver of Health Disparities: a Presidential Advisory from the American Heart Association," *Circulation* 142, no. 24 (2020): e454–68.

12. Kim Robin van Daalen et al., "Racial Discrimination and Adverse Pregnancy Outcomes: a Systematic Review and Meta-Analysis," *BMJ Global Health* 7, no. 8 (2022): e009227.

13. Bruce S. McEwen, "The Brain on Stress: Toward an Integrative Approach to Brain, Body, and Behavior," *Perspectives on Psychological Science* 8, no. 6 (2013): 673–75; Karen E. Smith and Seth D. Pollak, "Rethinking Concepts and Categories for Understanding the Neurodevelopmental Effects of Childhood Adversity," *Perspectives on Psychological Science,* 16, no. 1 (2021): 67–93.

14. Ibram X. Kendi, *Stamped from the Beginning: The Definitive History of Racist Ideas in America* (New York: Bold Type Books, 2016).

15. Joan Kaufman et al., "Transgenerational Inheritance and Systemic Racism in America," *Psychiatric Research and Clinical Practice* 5, no. 2 (2023): 60–73.

16. Diane Hughes et al., "Parents' Ethnic-Racial Socialization Practices: A Review of Research and Directions for Future Study," *Developmental Psychology* 42, no. 5 (2006): 748.

17. Eric Kyere and James P. Huguley, "Exploring the Process by Which Positive Racial Identity Develops and Influences Academic Performance in Black Youth: Implications for Social Work," *Journal of Ethnic & Cultural Diversity in Social Work* 29, no. 4 (2020): 286–304.

18. Riana Elyse Anderson and Howard C. Stevenson, "RECASTing Racial Stress and Trauma: Theorizing the Healing Potential of Racial Socialization in Families," *American Psychologist* 74, no. 1 (2019): 68.

19. Nia Heard-Garris et al., "Adolescents' Experiences, Emotions, and Coping Strategies Associated with Exposure to Media-Based Vicarious Racism," *JAMA Network Open* 4, no. 6 (2021): e2113522; Aisha Holder, Margo A. Jackson, and Joseph G. Ponterotto, "Racial Microaggression Experiences and Coping Strategies of Black Women in Corporate Leadership," *Qualitative Psychology* 2, no. 2 (2015): 164–80; Shawn C. T. Jones et al., "From "Crib to Coffin": Navigating Coping from Racism-Related Stress Throughout the Lifespan of Black Americans," *American Journal of Orthopsychiatry* 90, no. 2 (2020): 267–82.

20. Juan Del Toro and Ming-Te Wang, "Online Racism and Mental Health among Black American Adolescents in 2020," *Journal of the American Academy of Child & Adolescent Psychiatry* 62, no. 1 (2023): 25–36; Brendesha M. Tynes et al., "Race-Related Traumatic Events Online and Mental Health among Adolescents of Color," *Journal of Adolescent Health* 65, no. 3 (2019): 371–77.

21. Florida Department of Education, "Social Studies."

22. Kevin B. O'Reilly, "AMA: Racism Is a Threat to Public Health," American Medical Association, November 16, 2020, https://www.ama-assn.org/delivering-care/health-equity/ama-racism-threat-public-health; Maria Trent et al, "The Impact of Racism on Child and Adolescent Health," *Pediatrics* 144, no. 2 (2019): e20191765.

23. American Psychological Association, "Apology to People of Color for APA's Role in Promoting, Perpetuating, and Failing to Challenge Racism, Racial Discrimination, and Human Hierarchy in US, https://www. apa. org/about/policy/racism-apology.

CHAPTER 7

1. Abbie E. Goldberg and Roberto Abreu, "LGBTQ Parent Concerns and Parent–Child Communication About the Parental Rights in Education ('Don't Say Gay') in Florida," *Family*

Relations 73, no. 1 (2024): 318–39, https://doi.org/10.1111/fare
.12894; Nolan S. Kline et al., "Responding to 'Don't Say Gay'
Laws in the US: Research Priorities and Considerations for
Health Equity," *Sexuality Research and Social Policy* 19 (2022):
1397–402, https://doi.org/10.1007/s13178-022-00773-0.

2. Kimberle Crenshaw, "Demarginalizing the Intersection of
Race and Sex: A Black Feminist Critique of Antidiscrimina-
tion Doctrine, Feminist Theory and Antiracist Politics,"
University of Chicago Legal Forum 1989, no. 1 (1989): article 8,
http://chicagounbound.uchicago.edu/uclf/vol1989/iss1/8.

3. Dean Spade, "Intersectional Resistance and Law Reform,"
Signs 38, no. 4 (2013): 785–1060, https://doi.org/10.1086
/669574.

4. Darren L. Hutchinson, "Ignoring the Sexualization of Race:
Heteronormativity, Critical Race Theory and Anti-Racist
Politics," *Buffalo Law Review* 47, no. 1 (Winter 1999): 1–116,
http://scholarship.law.ufl.edu/facultypub/417.

5. D.-L. Stewart and Z. Nicolazzo, "High Impact of [Whiteness]
on Trans* Students in Postsecondary Education," *Equity &
Excellence in Education* 51, no. 2 (2018): 132–45, https://doi.org
/10.1080/10665684.2018.1496046.

6. Rigoberto Marquéz and Ed Brockenbrough, "Queer Youth
v. the State of California: Interrogating Legal Discourses on
the Rights of Queer Students of Color," *Curriculum Inquiry* 43,
no. 4 (2013): 461–82, https://doi.org/10.1111/curi.12021.

7. Antonio Duran, "Queer and of Color: A Systematic Review
on Queer Students of Color in Higher Education," *Journal of
Diversity in Higher Education* 12, no. 4 (2019): 390–400, https://
doi.org/10.1037/dhe0000084.

8. Ryan Schey, "Race and Queerness in the U.S. Schooling
System," in Oxford Research Encyclopedias, 2021, https://doi
.org/10.1093/acrefore/9780190264093.013.1372.

9. Shamari Reid, "Using a Queer of Color Critique to Work
Toward a Black LGBTQ+ Inclusive K–12 Curriculum," *Curriculum Inquiry* 53, no. 2 (2023): 105–25, https://doi.org/10
.1080/03626784.2022.2121594.

10. Alex C. Lange, Antonio Duran, and Romeo Jackson, "How
Whiteness Werqs in LGBTQ Centers," in *Critical Whiteness*

Praxis in Higher Education & Student Affairs: Considerations for the Pursuit of Racial Justice on Campus, ed. Zak Foste and Tenisha Tevis (Sterling, VA: Stylus, 2022), 155–71.

11. E. Brockenbrough, "Queer of Color Agency in Educational Contexts: Analytic Frameworks from a Queer of Color Critique," *Educational Studies* 51, no. 1 (2015): 28–44. https://doi.org/10.1080/00131946.2014.979929; Tadashi Dozono, "Queer of Color Literacies as Subversive Reading Practice: How Queer Students of Color Subvert Power in the Classroom," *Equity & Excellence in Education* 56, no. 1–2 (2023): 28–41, https://doi.org/10.1080/10665684.2022.2047412.

12. GLSEN, "Supporting LGBTQ Youth of Color," 2023, https://www.glsen.org/lgbtq-youth-color.

13. Debra Meyerson, "Radical Change, the Quiet Way," (2001, October), *Harvard Business Review*, https://hbr.org/2001/10/radical-change-the-quiet-way.

14. Rigoberto Marquéz, "Queer Latinx/o(x) Youth Education: A Community-Based Education Model to Queer of Color Praxis," *Equity & Excellence in Education* 52, no. 4 (2019): 396–408, https://doi.org/10.1080/10665684.2019.1696255.

15. Antonio Duran and Roland S. Coloma, "Queer Joy as an Affective Incitement to Queer and Trans Studies in Education," in *Bridging the Rainbow Gap: Possibilities and Tensions in Queer and Trans Studies in Education*, ed. Antonio Duran, Kamden K. Strunk, and Ryan Schey (Boston, MA: Brill, 2023), 109–24; Leonard D. Taylor, Dion T. Harry, and Reginald A. Blockett, "Black Queer Fugitivity: Agency, Language, and Digital Joy," *International Journal of Critical Media Literacy*, 3, no. 2 (2023): 105–19.

CHAPTER 8

1. James A. Coles and Darius Stanley, "Black Liberation in Teacher Education: (Re)Envisioning Educator Preparation to Defend Black Life and Possibility," *Northwest Journal of Teacher Education* 16, no. 2 (2021): 1–24.

2. Christina Sharpe, *In the Wake: On Blackness and Being* (Durham, NC: Duke University Press, 2016).

3. John E. Williams and Robert Ladd, "On the Relevance of Education for Black Liberation," *Journal of Negro Education* 47, no. 3 (1978): 266–82.

4. James A. Coles, "Black Lives, Too, Matter in Schools: An Exploration of Symbolic Violence Against Black Youth in America's Schools," *Urban Education Research and Policy Annuals* 4, no. 2 (2016): 17–33.

5. William H. McClendon, "Black Studies: Education for Liberation," *Black Scholar* 6, no. 1 (1974): 15

6. Darnell Ragland, "Truth-Telling as Decolonial Human Rights Education in the Movement for Black Liberation," *International Journal of Human Rights Education* 5, no. 1 (2021): 6.

7. Eduardo Bonilla-Silva, "The Linguistics of Color Blind Racism: How to Talk Nasty About Blacks Without Sounding 'Racist,'" *Critical Sociology* 28, no. 1–2 (2002): 41–64.

8. James A. Coles and Travis Powell, "A BlackCrit Analysis on Black Urban Youth and Suspension Disproportionality as Anti-Black Symbolic Violence," *Race Ethnicity and Education* 23, no. 1 (2020): 113–33; Damien M. Sojoyner, *First Strike: Educational Enclosures in Black Los Angeles* (Minneapolis: University of Minnesota Press, 2016).

9. Barbara Jones, "The Struggle for Black Education," in *Education and Capitalism: Struggles for Learning and Liberation*, ed. Joseph Bale and Susan Knopp (Chicago: Haymarket Books, 2012), 43.

10. Jones, "Struggle for Black Education," 47.

11. Eve Tuck, "Suspending Damage: A Letter to Communities," *Harvard Educational Review* 79, no. 3 (2009): 409–28.

12. David K. Chevannes and Juan R. Lopez, "Black Liberation and Political Education: The Valorizing of Afro-Ecuadorian Thought," *Comparative Education Review* 67, no. S1 (2023): S58.

13. Lerone N. Williams and Mohamed El-Khawas, "A Philosophy of Black Education," *Journal of Negro Education* 47, no. 2 (1978): 181.

14. Darnell Ragland, "Truth-Telling as Decolonial Human Rights Education in the Movement for Black Liberation," *International Journal of Human Rights Education* 5, no. 1 (2021): 5.

15. Ragland, "Truth-Telling," 20.

16. Ragland, 20.

17. Stokely Carmichael, "Toward Black Liberation," *The Massachusetts Review* 7, no. 4 (1966): 639.

18. Chevannes and Lopez, "Black Liberation and Political Education," S56.

19. James A. Coles, "Black Desire: Black-Centric Youthtopias as Critical Race Educational Praxis," *International Journal of Qualitative Studies in Education* 36, no. 6 (2023): 981–1002.

20. John E. King, "Education Research in the Black Liberation Tradition: Return What You Learn to the People," *Journal of Negro Education* 86, no. 2 (2017): 106.

21. Charles E. Cobb Jr., "Education for Liberation: Conference Keynote Address: Friday, 20 June 2014." *The Southern Quarterly* 52, no. 1 (2014): 32–42.

22. Cedric Haynes et al., "Black Deprivation, Black Resistance, and Black Liberation: The Influence of #BlackLivesMatter (BLM) on Higher Education," *International Journal of Qualitative Studies in Education* 32, no. 9 (2019): 1067–71.

23. Coles and Stanley, "Black Liberation in Teacher Education," 1–24.

24. Coles and Stanley, 7.

25. Coles and Stanley, 8.

26. Coles and Stanley, 10

27. King, "Education Research," 99

28. John E. King, "African People, Education for Liberation & Staying Human: Reflections on Walter Rodney and the Pan-African/Black Liberation Tradition," *Journal of Intersectionality* 2, no. 1 (2018): 31–40.

29. Williams and El-Khawas, "Philosophy of Black Education," 177–178.

30. William H. McClendon, "Black Studies: Education for Liberation," *The Black Scholar* 6, no. 1 (1974): 15.

31. Haynes et al., "Black Deprivation," 1067–71.

CHAPTER 9

1. Tyler Kingkade, "Moms for Liberty-Backed School Board Members Fire Superintendent, Ban Critical Race Theory."

NBCNews.com, November 17, 2022. https://www.nbcnews
.com/news/us-news/moms-liberty-berkeley-county-school
-board-superintendent-rcna57528; Stephen Sawchuck, "Local
School Boards Are Banning Critical Race Theory. Here's
How That Looks in 7 Districts," *Education Week*, August 25,
2021, https://www.edweek.org/leadership/local-school-boards
-are-also-banning-lessons-on-race-heres-how-that-looks-in-7
-districts/2021/08.

2. Rosemary Henze, Anne Katz, and Edmundo Norte, "Re-
thinking the Concept of Racial or Ethnic Conflict in Schools:
A Leadership Perspective," *Race, Ethnicity and Education* 3,
no. 2 (2000): 195–206; Gregory S. Jacobs, *Getting Around
Brown: Desegregation, Development, and the Columbus Public
Schools* (Columbus: Ohio State University Press, 1998).

3. Peter N. Kiang and Jenny Kaplan, "Where Do We Stand?
Views of Racial Conflict by Vietnamese American High-
School Students in a Black-and-White Context," *Urban
Review* 26, no. 2 (1994): 95–119.

4. Eve Ewing, *Ghosts in the Schoolyard: Racism and School Closings
on Chicago's South Side* (Chicago: University of Chicago Press,
2018).

5. Owen M. Fiss, "The Charlotte-Mecklenburg Case: Its
Significance for Northern School Desegregation," *University of Chicago Law Review* 38, no. 4 (1971): 697–709; Hugh
Macartney and John D. Singleton, "School Boards and
Student Segregation," *Journal of Public Economics* 164 (2018):
165–82; Rodney J. Reed, "School Boards, the Community,
and School Desegregation," *Journal of Black Studies* 13, no. 2
(1982): 189–206; Walter G. Stephan, "Brown and Intergroup
Relations: Reclaiming a Lost Opportunity," in *Commemorat-
ing Brown: The Social Psychology of Racism and Discrimination*,
ed. Glenn Adams et al. (Washington, DC: American Psychological Association, 2008).

6. James C. Bridgeforth, "Doing the Business of the District:
K–12 School Boards and Racial Crisis Leadership" (PhD
diss., University of Southern California, 2023).

7. Melanie Bertrand and Carrie Sampson, "Challenging Systemic Racism in School Board Meetings Through

Intertextual Co-Optation," *Critical Studies in Education* 63, no. 3 (2022): 323–39; Eupha Jeanne Daramola et al., "'On a Risky Slope of Democracy': Racialized Logics Embedded in Community–School Board Interactions," *Educational Evaluation and Policy Analysis* (2023), https://doi.org/10.3102 /01623737231175166.

8. Wendy Leo Moore, *Reproducing Racism: White Space, Elite Law Schools, and Racial Inequality* (Lanham, MD: Rowman & Little-field, 2008).

9. Martin Luther King Jr., *Letter from the Birmingham Jail.* (San Francisco: Harper San Francisco, 1994).

10. Deborah Land, "Local School Boards Under Review: Their Role and Effectiveness in Relation to Students' Academic Achievement," *Review of Educational Research* 72, no. 2 (2002): 229–78.

11. Abe Feuerstein, "Elections, Voting, and Democracy in Local School District Governance," *Educational Policy* 16, no. 1 (2002): 15–36.

12. Jonathan Collins. "Should School Boards Be In Charge? The Effects of Exposure to Participatory and Deliberative School Board Meetings," *Peabody Journal of Education* 96, no. 3 (2021): 341–55.

13. Chloe Banks, "Disciplining Black Activism: Post-Racial Rhetoric, Public Memory and Decorum in News Media Framing of the Black Lives Matter Movement," *Continuum* 32, no. 6 (2018): 709–20; Watoii Rabii, "One of the Good Ones: Rhetorical Maneuvers of Whiteness," *Critical Sociology* 48, no. 7–8 (2022): 1275–91.

14. Robert H. Anderson and Karolyn J. Snyder, "Leadership Training for the School Board Members: One Approach," *Education* 100, no. 3 (1980); Daniel W. Eadens, Frank D. Davidson, and Danielle M. Eadens, "Growing Evidence of the Value of School Board Training," *Education Leadership Review* 21, no. 1 (2020): 1–13; Janis Petronis, "Mandatory School Board Training: An Idea Whose Time Has Come?" ERIC, 1996, https://eric.ed.gov/?id=ED400625; Bobbie Plough, "School Board Governance and Student Achievement: School Board Members' Perceptions of Their Behaviors and Beliefs,"

Educational Leadership and Administration: Teaching and Program Development 25 (2014): 41–53.

15. Carrie Sampson and Melanie Bertrand. "'This is civil disobedience. I'll continue.': The Racialization of School Board Meeting Rules," *Journal of Education Policy* 37, no. 2 (2022): 226–46.

16. Daramola et al., "On a Risky Slope of Democracy."

CHAPTER 10

1. DEI Legislation Tracker, *The Chronicle of Higher Education*, July 14, 2023, https://www.chronicle.com/article/here-are -the-states-where-lawmakers-are-seeking-to-ban-colleges -dei-efforts.

2. Christopher F. Rufo, Ilya Shapiro, and Matt Beienburg, "Abolish DEI Bureaucracies and Restore Colorblind Equality in Public Universities," Manhattan Institute, 2023, https:// manhattan.institute/article/abolish-dei-bureaucracies-and -restore-colorblind-equality-in-public-universities.

3. Adrianna Kezar et al., *Shared Equity Leadership: Making Equity Everyone's Work* (Washington, DC: American Council on Education; Los Angeles: University of Southern California Pullias Center for Higher Education, 2021).

4. Megan Zahneis and Beckie Supiano, "Fear and Confusion in the Classroom: Vaguely Worded Legislation in Florida and Texas Is Already Affecting How Professors Teach," *Chronicle of Higher Education*, June 9, 2023, https://www.chronicle.com /article/fear-and-confusion-in-the-classroom.

5. Lorelle L. Espinosa et al., *Race and Ethnicity in Higher Education: A Status Report* (Washington, DC: American Council on Education, 2019).

6. Kezar et al., *Shared Equity Leadership*.

7. Rufo, Shapiro, and Beienburg, "Abolish DEI Bureaucracies."

8. For full definitions and more detail on these practices, please see Kezar et al., *Shared Equity Leadership*.

9. DEI Legislation Tracker.

10. Elizabeth Holcombe et al., *Leading for Equity from Where You Are: How Leaders in Different Roles Engage in Shared Equity Leadership* (Washington, DC: American Council on

Education; Los Angeles: University of Southern California Pullias Center for Higher Education, 2022); Elizabeth Holcombe et al., *Capacity Building for Shared Equity Leadership: Approaches and Considerations for the Work* (Washington, DC: American Council on Education; Los Angeles: University of Southern California Pullias Center for Higher Education, 2022); Elizabeth Holcombe et al., *Organizing Shared Equity Leadership: Four Approaches for Structuring the Work* (Washington, DC: American Council on Education; Los Angeles University of Southern California Pullias Center for Higher Education, 2021); Adrianna Kezar, Elizabeth Holcombe, and Darsella Vigil, *Shared Responsibility Means Shared Accountability: Rethinking Accountability Within Shared Equity Leadership* (Washington, DC: American Council on Education; Los Angeles: University of Southern California Pullias Center for Higher Education, 2022).

11. National Association of Diversity Officers in Higher Education, "Standards of Professional Practice for Chief Diversity Officers in Higher Education 2.0," 2020, https://nadohe .memberclicks.net/assets/2020SPPI/__NADOHE%20SPP2.0 _200131_FinalFormatted.pdf.

CHAPTER II

1. Fabiola Cineas, "Critical Race Theory and Trump's Executive Order on Diversity Training, Explained," *Vox*, September 24, 2020, https://www.vox.com/2020/9/24/21451220/critical -race-theory-diversity-training-trump; Ryan Cooper, "Changing the Subject," *The Week*, June 24, 2021, https://theweek .com/politics/1001865/critical-race-theory-george-floyd -protests.

2. Hailey Fuchs, "Trump Attack on Diversity Training Has a Quick and Chilling Effect," *New York Times*, October 13, 2020, https://www.nytimes.com/2020/10/13/us/politics/trump -diversity-training-race.html.

3. Donald L. Trump, "Executive Order 13950: Combating Race and Sex Stereotyping," United States Office of the Federal Register, September 22, 2020. https://www.hsdl .org/?abstract&did=844847, 60683.

4. Trump, "Executive Order 13950," 60683.

5. Trump, 60684

6. Anemona Hartocollis, "Princeton Admitted Past Racism. Now It Is Under Investigation," *New York Times*, September 18, 2020, https://www.nytimes.com/2020/09/17/us/princeton -racism-federal-investigation.html.

7. Anemona Hartocollis, "Justice Dept. Sues Yale, Citing Illegal Race Discrimination," *New York Times*, October 19, 2021, https://www.nytimes.com/2020/10/08/us/yale -discrimination.html.

8. Fuchs, "Trump Attack."

9. Kimberle Crenshaw [@sandylocks], "The Equity Gag Order Prohibits Agencies, Contractors, and Grant Recipients from Holding Diversity Training or Equity Programming that Discusses Topics," *Twitter*, December 23, 2020, https://twitter .com/sandylocks/status/1341925041567514625.

10. Sarah Schwartz, "MAP: Where Critical Race Theory Is Under Attack," *Education Week*, June 13, 2023, https://www.edweek .org/policy-politics/map-where-critical-race-theory-is-under -attack/2021/06.

11. Antar A. Tichavakunda, "A Critical Race Analysis of University Acts of Racial 'Redress': The Limited Potential of Racial Symbols," *Educational Policy* 35, no. 2 (December 23, 2020): 304–22, https://doi.org/10.1177/0895904820983031.

12. Divya Kumar, "Five Things to Know about Florida's New 'Intellectual Diversity' Law," *Tampa Bay Times*, June 26, 2021, https://www.tampabay.com/news/education/2021/06/26 /five-things-to-know-about-floridas-new-intellectual -diversity-law/.

13. Ana Ceballos, "State University Faculty, Students to Be Surveyed on Beliefs," *Tampa Bay Times*, June 22, 2021, https:// www.tampabay.com/news/florida-politics/2021/06/22/state -university-faculty-students-to-be-surveyed-on-beliefs/.

14. Ceballos, "State University Faculty."

15. "Governor Ron DeSantis Signs Legislation to Set the Pace for Civics Education in America," June 22, 2021, https:// www.flgov.com/2021/06/22/governor-ron-desantis-signs -legislation-to-set-the-pace-for-civics-education-in-america/.

16. Emma Pettit, "Legislating Viewpoint Diversity," Gale Academic OneFile, July 9, 2021, https://link.gale.com/apps /doc/A669680257/AONE?u=tamp44898&sid=bookmark -AONE&xid=fe788ec3.

17. Pettit, "Legislating Viewpoint Diversity."

18. Lindsey Ellis, "A Georgia Lawmaker Asked How Colleges Teach 'Privilege' and 'Oppression.' Here's How They Responded," *Chronicle of Higher Education*, February 19, 2021, https://www.chronicle.com/article/a-georgia -lawmaker-asked-how-colleges-teach-privilege-and -oppression-heres-how-they-responded; Eric Sturgis, "Georgia Colleges Address Concern About White Privilege Teaching," *Atlanta Journal Constitution*, February 12, 2021, https://www.ajc.com/education/ga-lawmakers-white -privilege-teaching-inquiry-sparks-anger-support /HCUEVLVXZFGEFOXLYMALH3GG5M/.

19. "Free Expression and Academic Freedom Syllabus Statement Frequently Asked Questions, Office of the Senior Vice President and Provost, Iowa State University," https://www .provost.iastate.edu/policies/syllabus-statement-faq.

20. "Governor DeSantis Announces Legislative Proposal to Stop W.O.K.E. Activism and Critical Race Theory in Schools and Corporations," December 15, 2021, https://www.flgov .com/2021/12/15/governor-desantis-announces-legislative -proposal-to-stop-w-o-k-e-activism-and-critical-race-theory -in-schools-and-corporations/.

21. "CS/HB 7: Individual Freedom", The Florida Senate, 2022, https://www.flsenate.gov/Session/Bill/2022/7.

22. "CS/HB 7: Individual Freedom."

23. Ben Brasch, "Judge Nixes Higher Education Portions of Florida's Stop WOKE Act," *Washington Post*, November 18, 2022, https://www.washingtonpost.com/nation/2022/11/17 /judge-nixes-higher-education-portions-floridas-stop-woke -act/.

24. Jim Saunders and Ryan Dailey, "Federal Judge Blocks Workplace Training Portion of DeSantis' 'Stop WOKE Act,'" *Miami Herald*, August 18, 2022, https://www.miamiherald.com

/news/politics-government/state-politics/article264659294
.html.

25. Erica Galluscio, "More than Meets the DEI," *PEN America*,
May 30, 2023, https://pen.org/more-than-meets-the-dei/.

26. "CS/CS/HB 999: Postsecondary Educational Institutions,"
The Florida Senate, 2023, https://www.flsenate.gov/Session
/Bill/2023/999.

CHAPTER 12

1. Derrick Bell, *Silent Covenants: Brown v. Board of Education and
the Unfulfilled Hopes for Racial Reform* (New York: Oxford University Press, 2004).

2. United States Department of Education, Institute for Education Sciences, State education practices, 2020, https://nces.ed
.gov/programs/statereform/tab1_2-2020.asp.

3. Congressional Research Service, "Membership of the
118th Congress: A Profile," November 13, 2023, https://
crsreports.congress.gov/product/pdf/R/R47470.

4. Loris Vezzali and Sofia Stathi, ed., *Intergroup Contact Theory:
Recent Developments and Future Directions* (New York: Routledge,
2017).

5. Frank Harris III and J. Luke Wood, "Racelighting: A Prevalent Version of Gaslighting Facing People of Color," *Diverse
Issues in Higher Education*, February 12, 2021, https://www
.diverseeducation.com/opinion/article/15108651/racelighting
-a-prevalent-version-of-gaslighting-facing-people-of-color.

6. Erica Frankenberg et al., "Harming Our Common Future:
America's Segregated Schools 65 Years After *Brown*" (Los
Angeles: UCLA Civil Rights Project, 2019), 4.

7. Kimberly Barsamian Kahn and Emma E. L. Money, "The Psychology of Race and Policing," in *Handbook of Issues in Criminal Justice Reform in the United States*, ed. Elizabeth Jeglic and
Cynthia Calkins (New York: Springer, 2022), 41–56.

8. Donna L. Hoyert, "Maternal Mortality Rates in the United
States, 2021," Centers for Disease Control and Prevention,
https://www.cdc.gov/nchs/data/hestat/maternal-mortality
/2021/maternal-mortality-rates-2021.htm.

9. Edward J. Smith and Shaun R. Harper, *Disproportionate Impact of K–12 School Suspension and Expulsion on Black Students in Southern States* (Philadelphia: University of Pennsylvania, Center for the Study of Race and Equity in Education, 2015).

10. Marianne Bertrand and Sendhil Mullainathan, "Are Emily and Greg More Employable Than Lakisha and Jamal? A Field Experiment on Labor Market Discrimination," *American Economic Review 94*, no. 4 (September 2004): 991.

11. Cyndy R. Snyder and Malaika R. Schwartz, "Experiences of Workplace Racial Discrimination among People of Color in Healthcare Professions," *Journal of Cultural Diversity* 26, no. 3 (Fall 2019): 96.

12. Katherine Schaeffer, "America's Public School Teachers Are Far Less Racially and Ethnically Diverse than Their Students," Pew Research Center, December 10, 2021, https://www.pewresearch.org/short-reads/2021/12/10/americas-public-school-teachers-are-far-less-racially-and-ethnically-diverse-than-their-students.

13. Maura Spiegelman, "Race and Ethnicity of Public School Teachers and Their Students," U.S. Department of Education, https://nces.ed.gov/pubs2020/2020103.pdf.

CHAPTER 13

1. kihana miraya ross, "Opinion: Call It What It Is: Anti-Blackness," *New York Times*, June 4, 2020, Opinion, https://www.nytimes.com/2020/06/04/opinion/george-floyd-anti-blackness.html.

2. Kasey Meehan and Jonathan Friedman, "Banned in the USA: State Laws Supercharge Book Suppression in Schools," April 20, 2023, https://pen.org/report/banned-in-the-usa-state-laws-supercharge-book-suppression-in-schools/.

3. UCLA Center for the Transformation of Schools, "Voices from the Classroom: Developing a Strategy for Teacher Retention and Recruitment," October 17, 2022, https://transformschools.ucla.edu/research/voices-from-the-classroom/.

4. Joel Spring, *Deculturalization and the Struggle for Equality: A Brief History of the Education of Dominated Cultures in the United States* (New York: Routledge, 2016).

5. Jaleel R. Howard, Cicely Bingener, and Tyrone C. Howard, "Essential Strategies for Inclusive Teaching," *ASCD*, December 6, 2021, https://www.ascd.org/el/articles/essential-strategies-for-inclusive-teaching.

6. Gholdy Muhammad, *Cultivating Genius: An Equity Framework for Culturally and Historically Responsive Literacy* (New York: Scholastic, 2020).

7. Janet Goodall and Caroline Montgomery, "Parental Involvement to Parental Engagement: A Continuum," *Educational Review* 66, no. 4 (October 2, 2014): 399–410, https://doi.org/10.1080/00131911.2013.781576; S. Wilder, "Effects of Parental Involvement on Academic Achievement: A Meta-Synthesis," *Educational Review* 66, no. 3 (July 3, 2014): 377–97, https://doi.org/10.1080/00131911.2013.780009.

8. Tyrone C. Howard and Rema Reynolds, "Examining Parent Involvement in Reversing the Underachievement of African American Students in Middle-Class Schools," *Educational Foundations* 22 (2008): 79–98.

9. Tyrone C. Howard, "Telling Their Side of the Story: African-American Students' Perceptions of Culturally Relevant Teaching," *Urban Review* 33, no. 2 (June 1, 2001): 131–49, https://doi.org/10.1023/A:1010393224120; Hersholt C. Waxman and Shwu-Yong L. Huang, "Classroom Instruction and Learning Environment Differences between Effective and Ineffective Urban Elementary Schools for African American Students," *Urban Education* 32, no. 1 (March 1, 1997): 7–44, https://doi.org/10.1177/0042085997032001002; Christy M. Byrd, "Does Culturally Relevant Teaching Work? An Examination from Student Perspectives," *SAGE Open* 6, no. 3 (July 2016), https://doi.org/10.1177/2158244016660744.

ABOUT THE EDITORS

Royel M. Johnson is a nationally recognized scholar and leader in higher education. He is associate professor and PhD program chair in the Rossier School of Education at the University of Southern California (USC). He is also the director of the National Assessment of Collegiate Campus Climates in the USC Race and Equity Center—the nation's leading tool for assessing campus racial climate. An expert and consultant on college access, student success, and organizational change for racial equity, Dr. Johnson has published over fifty peer-reviewed articles, chapters, and reports. His work appears in respected outlets such as the *Journal of Higher Education, Teachers College Record*, and *Education Administration Quarterly*. He has coedited three books: *Racial Equity on College Campuses: Connecting Research and Practice, Enacting Student Success: Critical and Alternative Perspectives for Practice*, and *Creating New Possibilities for the Future of HBCUs with Research*. Dr. Johnson's work has been funded by organizations such as the U.S. Department of Education, Spencer Foundation, and Chan Zuckerberg Foundation, totaling more than $6.3 million. He is also coeditor of *Educational Researcher*, the flagship journal for the American

Education Research Association (AERA). For his exemplary scholarly contributions, he was awarded the 2022 Early Career Award from AERA Division G, along with several other early-career honors from AERA, ACPA-College Educators International, and both of his alma maters, the University of Illinois at Urbana Champaign, and Ohio State University.

Shaun R. Harper is one of the nation's most highly respected racial equity experts. He is Provost Professor in the Rossier School of Education and the Marshall School of Business at the University of Southern California. In 2022, he was appointed University Professor, a distinction bestowed only to 26 of 4,700 USC full-time faculty members. Harper is also the Clifford and Betty Allen Chair in Urban Leadership, founder and executive director of the USC Race and Equity Center, and a *Forbes* contributor. He served as the 2020–2021 American Educational Research Association president and the 2016–2017 Association for the Study of Higher Education president. He was inducted into the National Academy of Education in 2021. Harper has published 13 books and over 100 academic papers. His research has been cited in more than 22,000 published studies across a vast array of academic fields and disciplines. The *New York Times, Washington Post, Wall Street Journal, Chronicle of Higher Education,* and several thousand other news outlets have quoted Harper and featured his research. He has been interviewed on CNN, ESPN, NBC News, and NPR. He also has testified twice to the United States House of Representatives and spoken at numerous White House convenings. The recipient of dozens of top honors in his field and four honorary degrees, Harper is currently ranked the nation's fourth-most influential professor in *Education Week*.

ABOUT THE CONTRIBUTORS

James Bridgeforth is a postdoctoral research fellow at the Community Schools Learning Exchange, a nonprofit consortium working directly with districts, municipal agencies, and community-based organizations to build and strengthen community school strategies. His research, recognized by the National Academy of Education/Spencer Foundation Dissertation Fellowship, critically examines issues of power, leadership, and governance, specifically attending to racism and anti-Blackness in K–12 schools. His scholarship can be found in academic journals such as the *Journal of School Leadership, Educational Administration Quarterly*, and *Educational Evaluation and Policy Analysis*, in addition to national media outlets such as *Education Week* and *The Hechinger Report*.

Ashley Burns Nascimiento is director at RALLY. A passionate communications strategist, Ashley focuses on racial and/or gender equity in education, health, housing, economic empowerment, and other social issues. From listening sessions with community matriarchs to focus groups in conservative rural communities, Ashley's work across the country helps fuel positive change through capacity building, community engagement, and messaging analysis. In short, she helps organizations and coalitions refine their voice to break through "noisy" landscapes and reach ambivalent audiences in unexpected ways. Prior to RALLY, Ashley led communications and media events for international product launches at Microsoft, Minecraft Education, Skype in the Classroom, LEGO, NASA, and various startups.

Justin A. Coles is an associate professor of social justice education in the department of Student Development at University of Massachusetts Amherst College of Education. Within the College, Dr. Coles serves as the inaugural director of Arts, Culture, and Political Engagement at the Center of Racial Justice and Youth Engaged Research (CRJ). Dr. Coles is a William T. Grant Theories of Blackness, Indigeneity, and Racialization in Research to Reduce Inequality in the Lives of Young People Writing Fellow. In 2023, Dr. Coles was inducted into the Martin Luther King Jr. Collegium of Scholars at Morehouse College.

Jessica T. DeCuir-Gunby is a professor of educational psychology in the University of Southern California's Rossier School of Education. She is an American Psychological Association Fellow for Division 15 (Educational Psychology) and an American Educational Research Association Fellow. DeCuir-Gunby is an associate editor for the *Review of Educational Research* and is serving on the editorial boards for *Contemporary Educational Psychology* and *Educational Psychologist*. Her research interests include the impact of race and racial identity development on the educational experiences of African Americans, critical race theory, mixed methods research, and emotions and coping related to racism.

Antonio Duran is an assistant professor of higher and postsecondary education in the Mary Lou Fulton Teachers College at Arizona State University. His research examines how historical and contemporary legacies of oppression influence college student development, experiences, and success. Connected to this central thread, he is also interested in how scholar-practitioners use the above knowledge in their practice. He uses critical frameworks (e.g., intersectionality, community cultural wealth, queer of color critique, quare theory, jotería studies) to complicate the field's understanding of racism, heterosexism, trans oppression, and other forms of marginalization on college campuses. Antonio completed his BA in English and American literature at New York University, MS in Student Affairs in Higher Education at Miami University, and PhD in Higher Education and Student Affairs at The Ohio State University.

Jarrett T. Gupton is an assistant professor of Higher Education and Student Affairs at the University of South Florida College of Education. He is a qualitative researcher focusing on college access, equity in education, higher education policy, and academic citizenship. He has authored multiple publications on homeless college students, food insecurity, and institutional capacity to support students experiencing basic needs insecurity. His current research explores anti-CRT legislation and higher education.

Elizabeth Holcombe is a senior postdoctoral research associate with the Pullias Center for Higher Education at the University of Southern California. Dr. Holcombe researches organizational change and leadership in higher education, with specific interests in leadership and change for diversity, equity, and inclusion (DEI), faculty development and workforce issues, undergraduate teaching and assessment, and STEM education. She has held a variety of roles in student affairs administration and was also an elementary school teacher. She holds a PhD from the University of Southern California; an MA from Teachers College, Columbia University; and a BA from Vanderbilt University.

Jaleel R. Howard is a doctoral candidate at UCLA in the School of Education and Information Studies. Jaleel's research endeavors focus on understanding the intricate web of social forces that impact the educational experiences and outcomes of chronically underserved students. Jaleel is currently an adjunct professor at Loyola Marymount University in the Education Psychology program.

Tyrone C. Howard is the Prizker Family Endowed Chair in the School of Education at UCLA. His research is focused on race, culture, and educational equity. He is the codirector of the UCLA Center for Transformation of Schools and the codirector of the UCLA Pritzker Center for Strengthening Children and Families. Professor Howard is a member of the National Academy of Education and president of the American Education Research Association.

Adrianna Kezar is Dean's Professor of Leadership and Wilbur-Kieffer Professor of Higher Education at the University of Southern California, and director of the Pullias Center for Higher Education. Dr. Kezar is a national expert of change and leadership in higher education. Her research has been used by national associations, government agencies, accreditation bodies, foundations, state systems, consortia, and individual campuses to forward change agendas and initiatives and design leadership development programs. She also regularly consults for campuses and national organizations related to her work on diversity/equity/inclusion, non-tenure-track faculty, STEM reform, collaboration, and governance.

Francesca López is the Waterbury Chair in Equity Pedagogy in the College of Education at The Pennsylvania State University. Her research program aims to inform policy makers, school leaders, and teacher educators about policies and classroom practices that can mitigate inequities. Her expertise includes asset-based pedagogy, bilingualism, and identity for Latinx youth. López's research has been funded by the American Educational Research Association Grants Program, the Division 15 American Psychological Association Early Career Award, the National Academy of Education/Spencer Postdoctoral Fellowship, the Chan Zuckerberg Initiative, the Institute for Educational Sciences, and others. She is a coeditor of the *Review of Educational Research.*

John Pascarella III is the chief academic officer of USC Race and Equity Center and professor of clinical education in the USC Rossier School of Education. As a leading expert in racial equity and teacher education, he has more than two dozen publications including peer-reviewed articles in *Cultural Studies ó Critical Methodologies, Educational Studies,* and *Taboo: The Journal of Culture and Education.* Dr. Pascarella has been a featured expert on *The Dr. Phil Show,* his op-eds have appeared in *Education Week,* and he has given over ninety invited talks and conference presentations dedicated to advancing equity-driven K–12 schools, colleges, and universities.

Elisa Serrano is a PhD student in the Curriculum & Instruction program at Penn State University. She holds a MA in rhetoric and composition from Texas State University and a BA in English from Texas A&M University. She is a research assistant and is currently involved in projects related to asset-based pedagogies and multilingual learners. Elisa's research interests, at a very general level, revolve around asset-based pedagogies, ethnic studies, and translanguaging pedagogical practices. More specifically, Elisa is interested in linguistic justice and restorative education for language-minority students, particularly for Latinx students, like herself.

Erica S. Silva is a school improvement specialist on the Quality Schools and Districts Team at WestEd, a nonpartisan research and service agency focused on achieving equitable learning outcomes for students across the country. She is also an adjunct assistant professor at USC Rossier School of Education. Prior to joining WestEd, Erica was the associate director of K–12 Programs at the USC Race and Equity Center. Erica began her career in education as a teacher and instructional specialist, working with educators on district-wide curriculum implementation, assessment development, technology integration, and culturally responsive pedagogy. She is a member of the Education Trust West's Educator Advisory Council and the K12 DE&I Advisory Board for Penguin Random House Education.

INDEX